LifeChange
S E R I E S

A NavPress Bible study on the book of

JOSHUA

NAVPRESS ®
A MINISTRY OF THE NAVIGATORS
P.O. BOX 35001, COLORADO SPRINGS, COLORADO 80935

The Navigators is an international Christian organization. Jesus Christ gave His followers the Great Commission to go and make disciples (Matthew 28:19). The aim of The Navigators is to help fulfill that commission by multiplying laborers for Christ in every nation.

NavPress is the publishing ministry of The Navigators. NavPress publications are tools to help Christians grow. Although publications alone cannot make disciples or change lives, they can help believers learn biblical discipleship, and apply what they learn to their lives and ministries.

Printed in the United States of America

9 10 11 12 13 14 15 16/99 98 97 96

FOR A FREE CATALOG OF
NAVPRESS BOOKS & BIBLE STUDIES,
CALL 1-800-366-7788 (USA)
or 1-416-499-4615 (CANADA)

CONTENTS

ACKNOWLEDGMENTS

The LIFECHANGE series has been produced through the coordinated efforts of a team of Navigator Bible study developers and NavPress editorial staff, along with a nationwide network of fieldtesters.

SERIES EDITOR: KAREN LEE-THORP

HOW TO USE THIS STUDY

Objectives

Most guides in the LIFECHANGE series of Bible studies cover one book of the Bible. Although the LIFECHANGE guides vary with the books they explore, they share some common goals:

1. To provide you with a firm foundation of understanding and a thirst to return to the book;

2. To teach you by example how to study a book of the Bible without structured guides;

3. To give you all the historical background, word definitions, and explanatory notes you need, so that your only other reference is the Bible;

4. To help you grasp the message of the book as a whole;

5. To teach you how to let God's Word transform you into Christ's image.

Each lesson in this study is designed to take 60 to 90 minutes to complete on your own. The guide is based on the assumption that you are completing one lesson per week, but if time is limited you can do half a lesson per week or whatever amount allows you to be thorough.

Flexibility

LIFECHANGE guides are flexible, allowing you to adjust the quantity and depth of your study to meet your individual needs. The guide offers many optional questions in addition to the regular numbered questions. The optional questions, which appear in the margins of the study pages, include the following:

Optional Application. Nearly all application questions are optional; we hope you will do as many as you can without overcommitting yourself.

For Thought and Discussion. Beginning Bible students should be able to handle these, but even advanced students need to think about them. These questions frequently deal with ethical issues and other biblical principles. They often offer cross-references to spark thought, but the references do not give

5

obvious answers. They are good for group discussions.

For Further Study. These include: a) cross-references that shed light on a topic the book discusses, and b) questions that delve deeper into the passage. You can omit them to shorten a lesson without missing a major point of the passage.

If you are meeting in a group, decide together which optional questions to prepare for each lesson, and how much of the lesson you will cover at the next meeting. Normally, the group leader should make this decision, but you might let each member choose his or her own application questions.

As you grow in your walk with God, you will find the LIFECHANGE guide growing with you—a helpful reference on a topic, a continuing challenge for application, a source of questions for many levels of growth.

Overview and Details

The study begins with an introduction to the book of Joshua. The key to interpretation is context—what is the whole passage or book *about?*—and the key to context is purpose—what is the author's *aim* for the whole work? In lesson one you will lay the foundation for your study of Joshua by asking yourself, "Why did the author (and God) write the book? What did they want to accomplish? What is the book about?"

In lessons two through fifteen you will analyze successive passages of Joshua in detail.

In lesson sixteen you will review Joshua, returning to the big picture to see whether your view of it has changed after closer study. Review will also strengthen your grasp of major issues and give you an idea of how you have grown from your study.

Kinds of Questions

Bible study on your own—without a structured guide—follows a progression. First you observe: What does the passage *say?* Then you interpret: What does the passage *mean?* Lastly you apply: How does this truth *affect* my life?

Some of the "how" and "why" questions will take some creative thinking, even prayer, to answer. Some are opinion questions without clearcut right answers; these will lend themselves to discussions and side studies.

Don't let your study become an exercise of knowledge alone. Treat the passage as God's Word, and stay in dialogue with Him as you study. Pray, "Lord, what do You want me to see here?" "Father, why is this true?" "Lord, how does this apply to my life?"

It is important that you write down your answers. The act of writing clarifies your thinking and helps you to remember.

Study Aids

A list of reference materials, including a few notes of explanation to help you make good use of them, begins on page 169. This guide is designed to include enough background to let you interpret with just your Bible and the guide. Still, if you want more information on a subject or want to study a book on your own, try the references listed.

Scripture Versions

Unless otherwise indicated, the Bible quotations in this guide are from the New International Version of the Bible. Other versions cited are the Revised Standard Version (RSV), the New American Standard Bible (NASB), the Good News Bible: Today's English Version (TEV), and the King James Version (KJV).

Use any translation you like for study, preferably more than one. A paraphrase such as The Living Bible is not accurate enough for study, but it can be helpful for comparison or devotional reading.

Memorizing and Meditating

A psalmist wrote, "I have hidden your word in my heart that I might not sin against you" (Psalm 119:11). If you write down a verse or passage that challenges or encourages you, and reflect on it often for a week or more, you will find it beginning to affect your motives and actions. We forget quickly what we read once; we remember what we ponder.

When you find a significant verse or passage, you might copy it onto a card to keep with you. Set aside five minutes during each day just to think about what the passage might mean in your life. Recite it over to yourself, exploring its meaning. Then, return to your passage as often as you can during your day, for a brief review. You will soon find it coming to mind spontaneously.

For Group Study

A group of four to ten people allows the richest discussions, but you can adapt this guide for other sized groups. It will suit a wide range of group types, such as home Bible studies, growth groups, youth groups, and businessmen's studies. Both new and experienced Bible students, and new and mature Christians, will benefit from the guide. You can omit or leave for later years any questions you find too easy or too hard.

The guide is intended to lead a group through one lesson per week. However, feel free to split lessons if you want to discuss them more thoroughly. Or, omit some questions in a lesson if preparation or discussion time is limited. You can always return to this guide for personal study later. You will be able to discuss only a few questions at length, so choose some for discussion and others for background. Make time at each discussion for members to ask about anything they didn't understand.

Each lesson in the guide ends with a section called "For the group." These sections give advice on how to focus a discussion, how you might apply the lesson in your group, how you might shorten a lesson, and so on. The group leader should read each "For the group" at least a week ahead so that he or she can tell the group how to prepare for the next lesson.

Each member should prepare for a meeting by writing answers for all of the background and discussion questions to be covered. If the group decides not to take an hour per week for private preparation, then expect to take at least two meetings per lesson to work through the questions. Application will be very difficult, however, without private thought and prayer.

Two reasons for studying in a group are accountability and support. When each member commits in front of the rest to seek growth in an area of life, you can pray with one another, listen jointly for God's guidance, help one another to resist temptation, assure each other that the other's growth matters to you, use the group to practice spiritual principles, and so on. Pray about one another's commitments and needs at most meetings. Spend the first few minutes of each meeting sharing any results from applications prompted by previous lessons. Then discuss new applications toward the end of the meeting. Follow such sharing with prayer for these and other needs.

If you write down each other's applications and prayer requests, you are more likely to remember to pray for them during the week, ask about them at the next meeting, and notice answered prayers. You might want to get a notebook for prayer requests and discussion notes.

Notes taken during discussion will help you to remember, follow up on ideas, stay on the subject, and clarify a total view of an issue. But don't let notetaking keep you from participating. Some groups choose one member at each meeting to take notes. Then someone copies the notes and distributes them at the next meeting. Rotating these tasks can help include people. Some groups have someone take notes on a large pad of paper or erasable marker board (preformed shower wallboard works well), so that everyone can see what has been recorded.

Pages 172-173 lists some good sources of counsel for leading group studies. The *Small Group Letter,* published by NavPress, is unique, offering insights from experienced leaders every other month.

The Promised Land

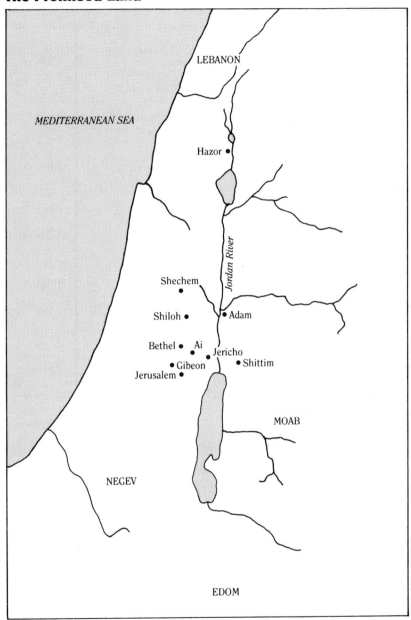

Timeline—Egypt to Babylon

(Dates are approximate, based on *The NIV Study Bible*)

Patriarchs (Genesis 12-50)	
Jacob (Israel) and family to Egypt (Genesis 46)	1876 BC
Exodus and Conquest (Exodus 1:1-Joshua 24:29)	
Moses leads Israelites out of Egypt and across the Red Sea	1446
Book of Joshua begins	1406
Southern and northern campaigns completed (Joshua 24:28)	1399
Joshua dies (Joshua 24:29)	1375
Judges (Judges 1-1 Samuel 9)	1375-1050
United Kingdom (1 Samuel 10-1 Kings 11)	
Saul becomes king of Israel	1050
David becomes king of Israel	1010
Solomon becomes king of Israel	970
Solomon dies; Israel and Judah split	930
Divided Kingdom (1 Kings 12-2 Kings 17)	930-722
Assyria destroys Israel	722
Babylonian captivity begins; the nobility of Judah are taken to Babylon	605
Jerusalem falls to Babylon; the rest of the Jews go into exile	586

INTRODUCTION

What Is Joshua?

Francis Schaeffer called the book of Joshua "a bridge, a link between the Pentateuch (the writings of Moses) and the rest of Scripture."[1] Precisely where the last book of Moses—Deuteronomy—leaves off in the tale of Israel's formation, the book of Joshua begins. And where Joshua closes, Judges takes up the story that points toward the New Testament and does not end until the book of Revelation.

Prophetic history

The Hebrew Bible is divided into three sections: the Law, the Prophets, and the Writings. Joshua through 2 Chronicles (minus Ruth) comprise the Former Prophets, and Isaiah through Malachi (minus Daniel) are the Latter Prophets. Christians sometimes call the Former Prophets the books of history, but we should remember that they are written as *prophecy*. This means that they are not intended to be thorough, scientific histories of the centuries they cover. Instead, their aim "is to present an interpretive (prophetical) history of God's dealings with his covenant people Israel, from the time of Moses' death until the Babylonian captivity." The stress here is *interpretive*. The human authors of these books were prophets guided by the Holy Spirit to unfold the fabric "that holds these events together and gives them their true meaning."[2] This prophetic history is chiefly about what *God did* in each event, and only secondarily about what human beings did. (For a compact example of prophetic history, see Joshua 24:2-13, which begins with the prophet's formula: "Thus saith the LORD God of Israel" [KJV].)

This is not to say that Joshua and the other human characters in the book are unimportant. But the supporting cast is always there to glorify the Star of the show. If we keep this in mind, we can better see why the author of Joshua details some scenes and brushes by others, and why he exhaustively records some matters that seem irrelevant to us.

11

The author

We've said "the author of Joshua" because we don't know who the human author was. Jewish tradition says that Joshua himself wrote all of the book except the accounts of his and Eleazar's deaths at the end. Modern critical scholars have dissected the book into sources from periods ranging from Joshua's time to six or eight hundred years later. Conservative scholars have suggested dates from just after Joshua's death to the time of David. The author apparently used some documents written by Joshua himself (8:32, 24:26), as well as survey records (18:9), and other sources (10:13). Many of the scenes have the vividness of eyewitness accounts; others seem to have the perspective of some distance. The book's thematic unity argues in favor of a single author, who may have been a younger contemporary of Joshua. Certainly the book's optimistic mood evokes either the time of Joshua or of David. But since the date of writing is not crucial to our understanding the message, we can set it aside for now.[3]

From Genesis to Joshua

Joshua records the fulfillment of promises God had been making for centuries. After Adam sinned, God began to prepare a family through whom He could redeem mankind. Genesis 1-11 records the early stages of that work and culminates in God's choice of one man, Abraham, to be the father of that family. In Genesis 12 and later, God makes three promises to Abraham: his children will inherit the land of Canaan (15:7); his children will become a great nation (12:2); and through his offspring will come a blessing to all the families of the earth (12:3, 22:18). The rest of Genesis tells the stories of Abraham, his son Isaac, and his grandson Jacob living as aliens in Canaan, never owning more than a burial plot for their dead but continuing to trust God's promises. The end of Genesis finds Jacob (also called Israel), his twelve sons, and their whole household moving to Egypt to escape a famine in Canaan. At every step, God has been at work shaping and protecting His people.

The book of Exodus begins several hundred years later. The descendants of Jacob-Israel have become slaves to a cruel Pharaoh of Egypt. But God intervenes ironically so that an Israelite named Moses is raised as a son of Pharaoh's daughter. As an adult he flees Egypt, and after forty years in the wilderness, God commissions him to lead Israel out of Egypt. God works miracles to free His people, including ten plagues on the Egyptians and the parting of the Red Sea. Through all this He proves that He, not the gods of Egypt, rules the forces of nature and the fates of men.

Moses leads Israel to Mount Sinai, where God makes a covenant—a royal treaty and an intimate pact—with His people. They swear to serve Him as His subjects, and He swears to rule them justly, protect them, and keep His promises to Abraham. God also gives His redeemed people a Law by which to live (this is recorded in Exodus, Leviticus, and Numbers). Then He sends them to take the land He has promised.

But after hearing of the formidable foes already living in Canaan, Israel is afraid to invade it. God is furious, and swears that none of that generation but the two who are willing to take Canaan will enter it. Those two are Joshua and Caleb. For thirty-eight more years, Israel is obliged to wander the desert between Egypt and Canaan (the book of Numbers tells of this wandering). Every Israelite over the age of twenty except Joshua, Caleb, and Moses dies. Finally Israel is allowed to reach the border of Canaan, on the plains of Moab east of the Jordan River. There Moses addresses Israel for the last time, recounting and reaffirming the covenant between God and Israel (these speeches comprise Deuteronomy). After this, Moses passes the leadership to Joshua and ascends Mount Nebo to die.

This is where the book of Joshua begins. The generation that refused to trust God's promises is now dead, and the new generation is at Canaan's doorstep. God is about to fulfill His promises to give Israel the land and make it a great nation. The third promise of Genesis 12—to bless all the earth through Israel—receives only glimpses in Joshua, for it will find its fullness only in Christ.

General Joshua

Even though the book is not mainly about the man Joshua, it is helpful to know a little about him. Right after the crossing of the Red Sea, Israel met its first enemy: Amalek. Joshua led the Lord's army in that battle (Exodus 17:8-16). When Moses and the elders of Israel ascended Mount Sinai to see God and to eat in His presence, Joshua was among them, and Joshua went still further up with Moses (Exodus 24:9-13). As early as this, Joshua saw God's power and glory. Joshua was also alone with Moses on the mountain when Aaron was below in the camp letting Israel fall into idolatry and debauchery (Exodus 32:17-35). Joshua had to watch the people decimated for this sin. Only Joshua stayed with Moses in the tabernacle when the Lord spoke with Moses face to face (Exodus 33:7-11).

Moses was Joshua's mentor, and the young man was naturally tempted to idolize his leader. But Moses taught Joshua that only the Lord's glory mattered, not his own. When Joshua was concerned that some elders were prophesying apart from Moses, the older man replied, "Are you jealous for my sake? I wish that all the LORD's people were prophets. . . !" (Numbers 11:24-29).

The real crux for Joshua came when he and eleven others went to spy out Canaan. Joshua and Caleb reported that the land was rich and ripe for taking by God's strength, but the other ten infected Israel with fear. The result was disaster: Israel was condemned to spend thirty-eight more years in the desert (Numbers 13:1-14:45). So Joshua served Moses until the time came for Israel to enter Canaan (Numbers 27:18-23, Deuteronomy 31:2-8,14-15). Joshua was equipped to lead Israel, for he was "filled with the spirit of wisdom because Moses had laid his hands on him" (Deuteronomy 34:9). God passed His Spirit from Moses to Joshua, having trained Joshua through Moses for forty years.

Interpreting Joshua

In lesson one you'll get a chance to decide for yourself what the book of Joshua is about and how it is relevant to you. You might want to consider some of the ways people have used the book in the past.

In Joshua, Israel conquers a piece of land by God's promise and power. God gives the right to possess it and the power to take it. The previous inhabitants are called wicked and have no rights to the land. Some Christians have seen this story as justification when they have conquered lands and exterminated or subjugated the natives. Today, many Christians challenge this application of the book. Likewise, "Some Israeli Jews today find in Joshua a mandate for repossessing Palestine without regard for Palestinians on the land, while others are deeply troubled by this interpretation."[4]

These are literal military applications. In addition, "Missionaries have used triumphalist language reminiscent of the Joshua story in speaking about 'occupying' and 'possessing' mission lands for Christ."[5] Some people find this language appropriate and inspiring, while others consider it insensitive to the people being evangelized.

Many people dislike the tone of Joshua on any level because God commands mass killings and seems to encourage hatred of foreigners. Moreover, "the long lists of cities and boundary lines [seem] boring."[6] The solution for some is to spiritualize the text: the book teaches individuals how to fight personal struggles against spiritual enemies, or how groups of believers should wage the Church's spiritual war. Some interpreters see Joshua conquering Canaan for Israel as a *type* (foreshadow) of Jesus conquering the earth for His people (both "Joshua" and "Jesus" reflect the same Hebrew name, *Yehoshua*.)

For others, the solution lies in defining the enemy. From the viewpoint of liberation theology, Joshua "tells us of

the faithfulness of God to his oppressed people;
the struggle for a place to live (land);
a successful movement of the disinherited against oppression, injustice, and tyranny;
the beginning of a new society based on justice, freedom, and loyalty."[7]

On this reading, the enemy is "the very powers that destroy life in our contemporary world," whether human, institutional, or spiritual.[8]

Where does this leave us? We begin with careful study of Scripture, acknowledging our biases but praying for God's guidance. Crucial biblical concepts for understanding Joshua are *covenant, rest, inheritance, redemption, warfare* and *the Kingdom of God.* In Old Testament times, God redeemed Israel, made a covenant with the people, promised rest in an inheritance, and led Israel to fight against enemies to claim an inheritance. In the New Testament we find a new covenant, a fuller redemption, a renewed promise of rest in our inheritance, and more warfare to establish the Kingdom of God. As we go through the book of Joshua, we will look at some of these key ideas in both Testaments to let you decide how to apply Joshua.

But we will begin with the book itself. For it is first of all an account of God's dealings with a particular people at a unique moment of history to achieve certain ends. As with all the Former Prophets, the tale is told so that "This is how you will know that the living God is among you" (Joshua 3:10).

1. Francis A. Schaeffer, *Joshua and the Flow of Biblical History* (Downers Grove, Illinois: Inter-Varsity Press, 1975), page 9.
2. Marten H. Woudstra, *The Book of Joshua* (Grand Rapids, Michigan: William B. Eerdmans Publishing Company, 1981), page 3.
3. For a survey of attempts to date the book, along with extensive footnotes, see Woudstra, pages 5-16.
4. E. John Hamlin, *Joshua: Inheriting the Land* (Grand Rapids, Michigan: William B. Eerdmans Publishing Company, 1983), page xi.
5. Hamlin, page xi.
6. Hamlin, page xi.
7. Hamlin, page xvi.
8. Hamlin, page xiii.

OVERVIEW

The Book of Joshua

You may have heard some of the exciting stories of Joshua—the crossing of the Jordan River, the battle of Jericho—but you may never have read the whole book before. You may have only a vague idea of its contents. This is the purpose of an overview: to give you a broad acquaintance with the themes and flavor of a book so that you can study each passage in light of the whole.

In this lesson you'll be reading most or all of Joshua at least once, as well as the Introduction on pages 11-15. If you are a slow reader or if you have never used a LIFECHANGE study guide before, you may want to take extra time for this overview. Also, be sure to look at the "How to Use This Study" section on pages 5-8.

1. Read the Introduction on pages 11-15. If you have any questions about it, write them here so that you will remember them. You can pursue answers later.

_____

_____

_____

_____

_____

_____

2. Now read the whole of Joshua once. Don't stop to untangle all the details or reflect on an interesting passage. Simply try to form a first impression of what the book is about. (You might want to skim chapters 12 through 21 just enough to get the gist of what they contain.) Keep questions 3 and 4 in mind as you do so.

3. What are your first impressions of the book? (For example, is it like a sermon, a series of stories, facts and figures, a logical argument to prove a point, poetry, or more than one of these? Is it dull or exciting or both in different places? Is it easy or confusing to follow? What mood does it seem to convey—upbeat, enthusiastic, depressing, cynical, angry, joyful . . . ?)

_____

_____

_____

_____

_____

_____

_____

4. Repetition is a clue to the ideas an author wants to emphasize. What are some of the words, phrases, and ideas that recur in the book of Joshua?

_____

_____

_____

_____

_____

_____

_____

5. An outline or chart often helps one see a book as a whole. To make a broad outline for an overview, begin by giving a title to each chapter.

1 _____

2 _____

3 _____

4 _____

5 _____

6 _____

7 _____

8 _____

9 _____

10 _____

11 _____

12 _____

13 _____

14 _____

15 _____

16 _____

17 _____

18 _____

19 _____

20 _____

21 _____

22 _____

23 _____

24 _____

6. Now group the chapters into larger sections. What is each of the following sections mainly about? What title would you give to each?

1:1-5:15 _____

_____

6:1-12:24 _____

_____

13:1-21:45 _____

_____

22:1-24:33 _____

_____

7. Finally, what would you say the book of Joshua as a whole is about? What themes (ideas that recur throughout the book) do you see? What do you think is God's purpose in giving His people this book?

_____

_____

_____

_____

_____

_____

_____

_____

8. Your overview may have suggested issues you want to explore and questions you want to answer as you study in more depth. If so, jot them down to serve as personal objectives for the rest of your study. What do you want to understand better by the time you are finished?

_____

_____

_____
_____
_____
_____

For Further Study:
a. Compare the book of Joshua to the New Testament book of Acts. Acts recounts how God began to conquer the world for His Kingdom, using His people as a kind of army empowered by His Spirit. Acts also pauses periodically to assess the progress made (Acts 2:41, 4:4, 6:7, 9:31, 19:20). How is Joshua like and unlike Acts?

b. Compare the books of Joshua and Revelation, and the missions of Joshua and Jesus. In what ways, if any, do you think Joshua foreshadows Jesus?

Study Skill—Application

Second Timothy 3:16-17 says, "All Scripture . . . is useful for teaching, rebuking, correcting and training in righteousness, so that the man of God may be thoroughly equipped for every good work." Paul also writes, "For everything that was written in the past was written to teach us, so that through endurance and the encouragement of the Scriptures we might have hope" (Romans 15:4), and "These things happened to them as examples and were written down as warnings for us . . ." (1 Corinthians 10:11). Therefore, when you study Joshua, you should keep asking yourself, "What difference should this passage make in my life? How should it make me want to think or act? How does it encourage, warn, correct, or set me an example?"

Application will require time, thought, prayer, and perhaps even discussion with another person. You may sometimes find it more productive to concentrate on one specific application, giving it careful thought and prayer, than to list several potential applications without really reflecting on them or committing yourself to them. At other times, you may want to list many implications that a passage has for your life. Then you can choose one or two of these to act or meditate upon.

9. In your first reading of Joshua, did you find any truths that are relevant to your life? If so, was there anything you would like to commit to memory, pray about, or act on? If so, write down your plans.

_____
_____

21

_____

_____

_____

_____

For the group

This "For the group" section and the ones in later
lessons are intended to suggest ways of structuring
your discussions. Feel free to select what suits your
group. The main goals of this lesson are to get to
know the book of Joshua as a whole and the people
with whom you are going to study it.

Worship. Some groups like to begin with prayer
and/or singing. Some share requests for prayer at
the beginning but leave the actual prayer until after
the study. Others prefer just to chat and have
refreshments for a while, then open the study with a
brief prayer for the Holy Spirit's guidance, and leave
worship and prayer until the end.

Warm-up. The beginning of a new study is a good
time to lay a foundation for honest sharing of ideas,
to get comfortable with each other, and to encourage a sense of common purpose. One way to establish common ground is to talk about what each person hopes to get out of your study of Joshua, and
out of any prayer, singing, sharing, outreach, or
anything else you might do together. You can also
share what you hope to give as well as get. If you
have someone write down each member's hopes and
expectations, then you can look back at these goals
later to see if they are being met. Goal-setting at the
beginning can also help you avoid confusion when
one person thinks the main point of the group is to
learn the Scripture, while another thinks it is to
support each other in daily Christian life, and
another thinks prayer or outreach is the chief
business.

How to Use This Study. Advise group members to
read the "How to Use This Study" section on pages
5-8 if they have not already done so. You might go
over important points that you think the group

22

should especially notice. For example, point out the optional questions in the margins. These are available as group discussion questions, ideas for application, and suggestions for further study. It is unlikely that anyone will have the time or desire to answer all the optional questions and do all the applications. A person might do one "Optional Application" for any given lesson. You might choose one or two "For Thought and Discussions" for your group discussion, or you might spend all your time on the numbered questions. If someone wants to write answers to the optional questions, suggest that he use a separate notebook. It will also be helpful for discussion notes, prayer requests, answers to prayers, application plans, and so on.

Invite everyone to ask questions about the "How to Use This Study" section.

Overview. Ideally, everyone should have read the whole book of Joshua and the Introduction before you meet together. However, some may not have done so, and others may not retain much of what they read quickly. So, ask a few questions to draw out the main points of the Introduction, such as:

1. What do you remember of Israel's history up to the point where the book of Joshua picks it up?
2. What do you know about Joshua the man?
3. Who are the main characters in the book? Who do you think is *the* main character? Why?
4. What is "prophetic history"? How is it helpful for you to know that Joshua is a prophetic book?

You may have to explain that Joshua is not necessarily prophetic in the sense of foretelling the future (although some people think it foreshadows Christ's work) but it is prophetic in the sense of interpreting history from a prophet's perspective. That is, the story is told with a focus on God.

Now go on to lesson one. Let group members share their first impressions of the book. Together, make a list of repeated words. What do they tell you about the ideas the author wanted to emphasize?

Compare your titles for each chapter and each larger section to those in some commentaries, study

23

Bibles, or handbooks. What similarities and differences do you see? Which approach do you find most helpful? Irving Jensen offers the following titles for four main divisions of the book:[1]

Preparation (1:1-5:15)
Conquest (6:1-12:24)
Inheritances (13:1-22:9)
Consecration (22:10-24:33)

What do you think of this view?

Next, make a list of the themes you can trace throughout the book. Try to come up with a clear, concise statement of what the book of Joshua is about, and another clear statement of what its purpose in the Bible might be.

Let everyone share questions he or she has about the book. Come back to them at the end to see if you have answered all of them.

Don't spend a lot of time on application in this lesson. Later lessons will attempt to guide those who are unsure how to apply Scripture to their lives. However, to give everyone something to think about, do share any ways you did find Joshua relevant to your lives.

Wrap-up. Briefly tell the group what to expect in lesson two. Whet everyone's appetite, and ask the group to think about any optional questions that you plan to discuss.

Worship. Many groups like to end with singing and/or prayer. This can include songs or prayers that respond to what you've learned in Bible study, or prayers for specific needs of group members. Some people are shy about sharing personal needs or praying aloud in groups, especially before they know the other people well. If this is true of your group, then a song and/or some silent prayer and a short closing prayer spoken by the leader might be an appropriate ending.

For instance, thank God for giving you this account of Israel's conquest of the land God had promised to give them. Thank Him for what it reveals about His nature and the whole story of His molding of a people for Himself. Thank Him for the opportunity to study His Word together.

1. Irving L. Jensen, *Rest-Land Won* (Chicago: Moody Press, 1966).

JOSHUA 1:1-18

Marching Orders

Moses is dead. Suddenly, Joshua is the man with primary responsibility, under God, to lead Israel into the promised land. The enemies that frightened Israel out of Canaan forty years ago are as fierce as ever, but the Lord is also the same God who brought Israel out of Egypt and safely through the desert.

Before beginning the questions in this lesson, read 1:1-18 carefully. Observe each detail. Try to put yourself into the place of Joshua. Then read the chapter again, putting yourself into the shoes of the Israelites listening to him. Ask God to enable you to understand what He is saying, and what He is saying to you personally, in this passage.

1. What does God tell Joshua to do in 1:1-9? List all the commands you can find.

_____

_____

_____

_____

_____

_____

_____

For Thought and Discussion: Why do you think God repeats "Be strong and courageous" so often in chapter 1?

2. What does God promise Joshua in these verses?

_____

_____

_____

_____

_____

_____

_____

_____

Moses the servant of the LORD . . . Moses' aide
(1:1). In the royal terminology of the ancient Near East, a king's "servant" was a trusted, honored envoy or minister.[1] Only the Lord's most intimate representatives are called His servants in the Old Testament. Moses receives this title often.

At the beginning of the book of Joshua, Joshua is only "Moses' aide." It is an honorable position; the word "denotes personal service from man to man" performed voluntarily or by a calling.[2] However, it is a subordinate role. At his death (24:29), Joshua is at last called "the servant of the LORD"—by that time he has earned the title.

Your territory (1:4). See the map on page 9. ***The desert*** ("wilderness" in KJV) borders Israel on the south and east, including the Negev, Edom, and the land east of Moab. ***Hittite*** was a loose name for the natives of Canaan. ***The Great Sea*** is the Mediterranean Sea. Israel only approached these outer boundaries briefly under David and Solomon.[3]

Inherit (1:6). Taking possession of the promised inheritance is a theme of the book of Joshua. The words *inheritance* and *inherit* (Deuteronomy 1:38, 12:10) imply that Israel has a claim on the land over its former inhabitants, that this claim persists through generations, and that it is apportioned to Israel like a father's legacy to a son or like a king's grant to a loyal subject.[4] Israel has a right to the land not because of its own deserving but because He who owns the land has chosen to give it to Israel (Leviticus 25:23). He is throwing the former tenants off because of their wickedness (Genesis 15:16, Deuteronomy 9:1-5; compare Matthew 21:33-46).

Words related to inheritance are *portion* and *lot* or *allotment* (15:1, 18:6-7). On one level, Israel's portion or inheritance is physical land. On a deeper level, however, the Lord is Israel's inheritance, and each person and tribe has a "share" (22:25) in Him. Psalm 16:5-6 expresses this idea.

Israel's inheritance is the Kingdom of God. For the Israelites, this was a piece of real estate and a political nation governed by God. For Christians, it is something wider. Jesus Christ is the King. His subjects live already in His Kingdom, yet they await the full presence of His Kingdom when He returns.

Law (1:7). *Torah* in Hebrew. This is wider than law in the English sense. It includes all of God's revealed word in Genesis through Deuteronomy: His self-revelation, His deeds on His people's behalf, and His covenant that includes rules for living. To act according to God's Law is to act in accord with His commands, His deeds, and His revealed character.

The Reubenites, the Gadites, and the half-tribe of Manasseh (1:12). Israel was divided into twelve tribes according to the twelve sons of Jacob (whom God renamed Israel). The tribe of Joseph was also divided in two according to Joseph's two sons, Ephraim and Manasseh. Because Joseph saved his family from famine, Jacob adopted Joseph's sons as his own, and their descendants became full tribes (Genesis 48:1-22).

At the end of the wilderness wandering, as Israel was approaching Canaan, the nation defeated some hostile Amorites east of the Jordan. The tribes of Reuben and Gad, and half of the tribe of Manasseh, liked that eastern land so

For Further Study: Using a concordance or topical Bible, study the idea of inheritance or the Kingdom of God in the New Testament. What is our inheritance in Christ? What has God promised us, and what has He not promised us? To what extent can we possess our inheritance in this life, and to what extent must we wait until after resurrection?

27

For Thought and Discussion: a. Why was it so important that all Israel fight for the land together?

b. How is this relevant to us as Christians (Romans 12:3-8; 1 Corinthians 12:12-26; Philippians 1:27-30, 2:1-4)? What commands and truths must we "Remember" (Joshua 1:13) about each other?

c. How is this relevant to you personally?

much that they asked Moses to allot it to them as their inheritance. Moses agreed, on the condition that the warriors of those tribes would help Israel conquer Canaan (Numbers 32). The author of Joshua stresses repeatedly that *all* Israel fought together (1:2; 3:1,7; 6:3; 8:1; etc.).

Rest (1:13,15). "Security from disruption or enemy attack on land which has been given as an inheritance (Deuteronomy 12:9-10)."[5] Rest is a sign of God's presence (Exodus 33:14) and provision (Joshua 1:13). Like all the blessings God promises Israel, rest is forfeited if the people sin (Deuteronomy 28:1-68).

Through Joshua, the Lord gave Israel temporary, limited, but real rest from its enemies (Joshua 21:44, 22:4, 23:1). But because the people fell into idolatry and other disobedience after Joshua's death, Israel suffered repeatedly from attack and insecurity for several hundred years (Judges 2:6-23). When David became king and led Israel to be loyal to the Lord, the nation enjoyed rest again (2 Samuel 7:1). Under godly kings after him there was rest (1 Kings 5:4; 2 Chronicles 14:2-6, 20:30), but the bad kings were responsible for sin, internal disorder and discontent, and ultimately national destruction and exile.

According to Psalm 95:7-11, the wilderness generation failed to enter God's rest in Canaan because they faithlessly tested God's power and love at Meribah and Massah (Exodus 17:1-7, Numbers 20:1-13). Hebrews 3:7-4:11 applies this Psalm and the story of Joshua to Christians, and shows us how the idea of rest applies to us. Rest comes to those who come to Jesus (Matthew 11:28-29), who believe in Him, and who obey Him (Hebrews 4:3,11).

3. What role will God have in the conquest of the land He has promised? (Notice a repeated idea in Joshua 1:2-3,5,9,11,13-15.)

_____

_____

_____

_____

_____

4. What will be Israel's responsibilities in obtaining the land (1:2,7-18)?

_____

_____

_____

_____

_____

Study Skill—Cross-references

In the word definitions above, you can see that other passages of Scripture are enormously helpful in understanding a given passage. A concordance (see page 170) can help you trace a key word like *inheritance* or *rest* through the Bible. Seeing how these words are used in the New Testament will show you what they mean, and this in turn will help you apply them to yourself.

---

5. What do the following passages tell you about the inheritance God has promised Christians? (Look at as many as you like.)

Matthew 5:3,5 _____

_____

Matthew 19:29-30 _____

_____

Matthew 25:34-40 _____

_____

For Thought and Discussion: Does Joshua 1:1-18 suggest that Israel's inheritance was by works, by grace, or both? Explain your answer.

Optional Application: a. What promises has God given you (such as about forgiveness, your inheritance, eternal life)? How do you feel about them?

b. What commands has He given you (such as about sin, love, money, being a witness)? How do you feel about them?

c. How well are you carrying out His commands and acting on His promises? How can you improve?

Optional Application: How strong and courageous are you as you face the challenge to possess your inheritance? What motivates and demotivates you? Pray about this.

For Thought and Discussion: Why are meditating on and obeying God's Word crucial to succeeding in possessing our inheritance? (See Joshua 1:7-8, Matthew 7:24-27, Hebrews 4:8-13.)

Optional Application: a. How is 1:16-18 an example for you in dealing with your leaders?

b. Pray for your leaders, that they may be strong and courageous and careful to meditate on and obey God's words.

Romans 8:15-17 _____

_____

_____

_____

Philippians 3:20-21 _____

_____

_____

_____

1 Peter 1:4, 2:9-10 _____

_____

_____

_____

Revelation 21:1-7 _____

_____

_____

_____

_____

6. Read Hebrews 3:12-4:11. What rest has God promised us?

_____

_____

_____

_____

_____

_____

7. If Joshua 1:1-18 is a clue, what role do you think God has in seeing that we inherit what He has promised?

_____

_____

_____

_____

8. From Joshua, what do you think our responsibilities are in attaining our inheritance? (*Optional:* See Hebrews 4:11, 6:12.)

_____

_____

_____

_____

_____

9. According to the orders he received from his Commander in Chief, Joshua instructed all Israel to *prepare* (Joshua 1:10-11) and the eastern tribes to *remember* (1:12-15).
   How did the people respond (1:16-18)?

_____

_____

_____

_____

_____

For Thought and Discussion: a. What authorized Israel to claim and begin fighting for Canaan?

b. How can we decide whether we are authorized to begin some enterprise? What warrants us to start acting in faith?

For Thought and Discussion: How do Christians prepare to take possession of what God has promised them?

Optional Application: Take time each day this week to meditate on some aspect of your inheritance from question 5. Thank God for this promise and for the extent to which He has already given you what He has promised. Ask Him for the strength, courage, and wisdom to do whatever is necessary to lay hold of this inheritance. If your meditation and prayer suggest any specific action you need to take, write it down and do it.

10. What one truth from this lesson seems most relevant to your life right now? (Is there a sin to avoid, a promise to act on, an example to follow, a command to obey, or knowledge about God to respond to?)

_____

_____

_____

_____

_____

11. How do you fall short or want to grow in this area?

_____

_____

_____

_____

_____

12. What action can you take, including prayer, to begin putting this truth into practice this week? Think of at least one concrete step you can take.

_____

_____

_____

_____

_____

_____

13. If you have any questions about 1:1-18 or the material in this lesson, write them down so that you will remember to seek answers.

_____

_____

_____

_____

_____

For the group

Worship.

Warm-up. People often come to group meetings with their minds still buzzing from the day's business. Beginning in prayer and worship can help you focus on God and His Word. Another way to aid the group to shift gears is to open with a short ice-breaker or warm-up question related to the topic of the study. For example, ask each person to name one thing God has promised him or her without looking at a study guide. Give everyone a moment to think, then move quickly around the room for responses. Don't take time to discuss answers, since this question is meant only to get the mental juices flowing.

Read aloud. It is a good idea to begin a study by reading the passage at hand aloud. Some people may be present who have not done the lesson questions, and others may appreciate having their memories refreshed. Ask someone to read 1:1-18 with expression, almost as though he or she were acting out the parts of God and Joshua. If you like, assign the roles of God, Joshua, and a narrator to different people.

Summarize. Before plunging into the details of the chapter, ask someone to summarize briefly what it is about. A quick overview will help you see the sweep of a story and study the details in context.

Questions. In later lessons you will find Study Skills to help you interpret and apply Old Testament narratives. The main guides in this lesson are the New Testament cross-references on inheritance and rest. These are so detailed because you will want to use them as standards for application throughout your study of Joshua. To organize your discussion, you might do the following:

    1. Discuss what the actual text of Joshua 1:1-18 says (questions 1-4, 9). It is tempting for

33

a. Who or what does Ephesians 6:12 suggest are our enemies in the battle for the Kingdom of God—people, institutions, demons, ideas, inner habits, others? Do some research to find various views.

b. If we overthrow wicked people or institutions, do we always, sometimes, or never further the Kingdom? Give reasons for your opinion.

Christians to immediately allegorize or spiritualize Old Testament stories. Help the group to see 1:1-18 first of all as a unique event in history. (Has God ever given a people land the way He gave it to Israel?) Try to envision the scene, feel Joshua's feelings, and perceive what the Lord was saying about Himself when He said and did these things.

2. Ask each person to explain what one or two of the cross-references in questions 5 and 6 reveal about our inheritance and rest. Also, discuss what the definitions of inheritance and rest on pages 26 and 28 add. How is our inheritance like and unlike Israel's? How should this affect the ways we apply Joshua?

3. Discuss what you learn about God from 1:1-18 and how the chapter is relevant to you.

4. Share your plans for specific action this week. If some members are unfamiliar with how to apply Scripture, let the group make some suggestions without being pushy.

Summarize. After studying in detail, go back and summarize what the passage is about. Then summarize how it is relevant to you.

Wrap-up.

Worship. Thank God for promising you rest in an inheritance. Thank Him for all the things you have learned about your inheritance. Thank Him for His Word that guides you in possessing what He is graciously giving you. Ask Him to enable each of you to do your part in laying hold of your inheritance.

Inheritance in Ephesians

J. Sidlow Baxter uses the book of Ephesians to explain the similarities and differences between Israel's inheritance and our own.[6] He observes:

1. God promised Israel material blessings in an earthly place—Canaan (Genesis 13:14-17, Deuteronomy 28:1-14). He promises us spiritual blessings in a heavenly place (Ephesians 1:3-4).

2. Just as Israel's inheritance was "predestined" (promised long before it was received), so ours was predestined for us before the creation of the world (Ephesians 1:3-5).

3. As Joshua led Israel into its inheritance

(continued on page 35)

34

(continued from page 34)

(Joshua 1:6, 11:23), so Christ leads us into ours (Ephesians 1:18-22, Colossians 1:18).

4. As Israel received Canaan by grace, without earning it through prior goodness (Deuteronomy 9:1-5), so we receive our inheritance by grace (Ephesians 2:5-8).

5. Israel's possession of Canaan revealed to all peoples on earth that the Lord is supreme (Deuteronomy 28:10, Joshua 4:24). Likewise, our possession of spiritual riches in Christ proves God's wisdom and power to the principalities and powers in the heavens (Ephesians 3:8-10).

6. Israel had to fight for Canaan by God's power against evil enemies (Deuteronomy 9:1-5, Joshua 11:16-20). Likewise, through God's power we must fight evil spiritual enemies "in the heavenly realms" for our inheritance (Ephesians 6:10-18).

Notice that all these passages in Ephesians refer to "the heavenly realms." We have a heavenly leader to fight heavenly (spiritual, unearthly) foes to win a heavenly inheritance. But Ephesians also makes it clear that the foes, the leader, and the battle are present with us here and now. And our Canaan—the Kingdom of God, eternal life, riches in Christ—is in part available to us here and now as well (Luke 17:20-21, Ephesians 1:3).[7]

---

1. *The NIV Study Bible,* edited by Kenneth Barker (Grand Rapids, Michigan: Zondervan Corporation, 1985), pages 1074, 1076.
2. Woudstra, page 57.
3. Woudstra, page 60.
4. Woudstra, pages 61-62.
5. Hamlin, page 12.
6. J. Sidlow Baxter, *Explore the Book*, volume 1 (Grand Rapids, Michigan: Zondervan Corporation, 1966), pages 247-252.
7. The term "heavenly" in Ephesians confuses some people. If we think of the heavens as the realm of God, we may not understand enemies in the heavens (6:12). The fact that both God's angelic subjects and His demonic enemies reside in the heavens tells us that this is the spiritual realm, the abode of all that is not physical and earthly. This spiritual realm has a great deal of interest and involvement in the earthly realm.

JOSHUA 2:1-24

Reconnaissance in Jericho

Joshua has his orders: enter and take the land God
will give you. But instead of immediately crossing
the Jordan to Jericho, Joshua sends a scouting party
to gather intelligence. This mission will have unex-
pected but far-reaching consequences.

    Read 2:1-24. Observe as many details as possi-
ble, and ask God to tell you what He wants to say
through this episode.

1. After carefully reading a chapter, it is a good
   idea to step back and see if you understand
   what is going on. Basically, what happens in
   2:1-24?

   _____

   _____

   _____

   _____

   _____

   _____

   _____

   _____

   _____

Study Skill—Interpreting Old Testament Narratives

A narrative is a story. When we read a biblical narrative, we are reading part of the true story about God as He revealed Himself to people over centuries. Here are some principles for interpreting any biblical narrative, particularly Old Testament ones as in Joshua:

1. Not every episode in Israel's history is meant to teach an individual moral lesson. Sometimes a story is significant only as part of the whole history of God's dealings with Israel.

2. Narratives record what happened, not necessarily what ought to happen every time. So again, a particular story may not have its own moral. (For example, the rites and the meeting in Joshua 5, and the lots cast to divide the land in chapters 14-21, are not events to be repeated in just the same way.)

3. Not every detail of a narrative has deep significance. (The flax in 2:6 probably doesn't.) The point may be in the overall message. However, the point may not be clear until we carefully observe many details.

4. Narratives often teach by clearly implying something without actually stating it. However, we should be wary of teachers who see "hidden" meanings that other Christians do not see (such as symbolism in the precise way Rahab hides the spies or in the three days they spend in the hills).

5. "*All* narratives are selective and incomplete. Not all the relevant details are always given (see John 21:25). What does appear in the narrative is everything that the inspired author thought important for us to know." (We must be content with our curiosity unsatisfied about how God stopped the Jordan's flow in 3:14-17 or about how each city in chapters 10-11 was captured.)

6. "Narratives are not written to answer all our theological questions. They have particular, specific limited purposes and deal with certain issues, leaving others to be dealt

(continued on page 39)

(continued from page 38)
with elsewhere, in other ways." (We should
not try to make Joshua into a thorough handbook for living the victorious Christian life or
being the ideal Christian leader.)
    7. God is the main character (the hero)
of all biblical narratives. The human beings
are always secondary characters in a story
about what God did.[1]

2. The Lord had repeatedly promised to *give* the
land to Israel (1:2-3,6,13,15). Was Joshua faith-
less, then, to send spies to scout the quarry?
Why or why not?

_____

_____

_____

_____

_____

Jericho (2:1). This was the first strategic fortress on
the edge of Canaan. It stood on a large and fertile plain just west of the Jordan. Jericho
guarded the foot of the road that climbed steeply
up the Judean hills. In order to gain control of
Canaan, an army had to take Jericho to reach
the road, then take the fortresses that guarded
the high ground at the top of the road. From
there, an army could launch strikes to the south
and north of Canaan. During these campaigns,
the invaders could leave a safe camp on the
plains of Jericho. This is just what Joshua did.[2]

Prostitute (2:1). Some early Jewish sources call her
an "innkeeper," since the Hebrew word used
here also had that meaning. However, the Greek
of Hebrews 11:31 and James 2:25 means clearly
"prostitute." Both New Testament writers chose
to stress Rahab's occupation to highlight her
actions.
    The story does not suggest that the spies

39

employed Rahab at her trade. Rather, a prostitute's house was a normal place for men to come and go, so the spies were less likely to attract attention entering there. Also, a marginal member of Canaanite society like Rahab was more likely to harbor enemies than most people. Then as now in Asia and the Near East, poor families often supplemented their incomes by making their daughters prostitutes for the wealthy.[3] Rahab had little reason to be loyal to the lords of Jericho.

King (2:2). Canaanite society was divided into sharp classes. At the top were "kings," who were really lords of individual walled fortresses called "cities." The kings owed allegiance and service to the Egyptian pharaoh, who technically ruled Canaan. In return, the kings received authority over their cities and the surrounding land. In practice, Egypt left the kings with a free hand to run their territories, and the kings did so ruthlessly.

Under each king, and living with him in the city, was a class of nobles. These traded their allegiance and service to the king for status and land. Alongside the nobles were the priests. Again, the king gave them land and status, and they supported him.

Below these was about ninety-eight percent of the population. Slaves and tenant farmers worked the lands owned by the king, nobles, and priests. They lived in villages near the city. Artisans, too, lived in the villages and served primarily the overlords. In villages further from the city lived free farmers and shepherds. These paid taxes to the king and so were "subject to debt slavery and forced labor."[4] Outside this system were groups of outlaws— "former tenant farmers or slaves" who sometimes became mercenaries for the king but more often plagued him.[5]

When we read of cities in Joshua, we must remember that they were really fortresses with mud brick walls many feet thick. Archaeologists have found that Jericho covered only about nine acres.[6] It measured about 225 by 80 meters. Jerusalem in David's time measured 400 by 100 meters, and Shechem was 230 by 150 meters.[7] A city was mainly the home of the upper classes, although the villagers could crowd in when invaders attacked.

Kindness (2:12). The Hebrew word *hesed* is a key word in Scripture. It is often translated "love," "lovingkindness," or "unfailing love" elsewhere. It expresses the love between people who are bound by a covenant: God's favor towards His covenant people regardless of their deeds; or the care and loyalty God's people are supposed to show for each other.[8]

Kindly and faithfully (2:14). Kindness and faithfulness is "the standard expression for acts done . . . in connection with covenant agreements"[9] (Genesis 24:27,49; 32:10). Rahab and the spies have made a covenant in the Lord's name (2:12). In fact, Rahab is moving toward joining God's covenant people.

Scarlet cord (2:18). As the blood on the doorposts showed the angel of death which houses' inhabitants to spare in Egypt (Exodus 12:13, 22-23), so this red marker showed Israel which house's inhabitants to spare in Jericho. Thus, the scarlet cord recalled the Passover lamb, whose blood covered and protected the covenant people. That blood was a type (foreshadowing symbol) of Christ's blood, which covers our sin and protects us from destruction (Hebrews 9:11-14, 1 Peter 1:19).

---

3. Read Hebrews 11:1-2,31 and James 2:25-26. What lessons do these New Testament letters draw from Joshua 2?

Hebrews _____

_____

_____

_____

James _____

_____

41

For Thought and Discussion: a. What did Rahab risk by lying to the king's messengers? What did she have to lose?

b. What did she have to gain? From the story, what do you think motivated Rahab to take the risk?

c. What might you have to risk to serve God's people and God's plans? What do you have to gain?

For Thought and Discussion: Do you think Rahab was wrong to lie? (*Optional:* See Exodus 1:15-21, Ephesians 4:25.) What would you have done in Rahab's place, and why?

4. What was Rahab's "faith"? What did she believe about the Lord, and why (Joshua 2:8-11)?

5. How did her beliefs affect her deeds (2:2-7,12-21)?

6. a. What became of Rahab and her family when Israel finally took Jericho (6:17-25)?

b. God had commanded that all the Canaanites must be destroyed because of their wickedness toward each other and their rebellion against Him (Deuteronomy 7:1-5, 9:1-5). Why was the family of Rahab the pagan prostitute

42

saved from destruction? What does this tell you about God?

_____

_____

_____

_____

_____

_____

7. Matthew mentions only four women in his genealogy of Jesus. What is significant about Matthew 1:5a, and why is it significant?

_____

_____

_____

_____

_____

8. The spies learned some information on their mission (2:9-11,23-24). Why was it important for Joshua to hear this? (Recall 1:9.)

_____

_____

_____

_____

_____

9. What points do you think the inspired author is trying to make by including Rahab's story in his account? What does the story of the pagan prostitute contribute to the whole of Joshua?

_____

_____

_____

For Thought and Discussion: Do you think the king's messengers were naive not to search Rahab's house? Why or why not? What protected the spies?

For Thought and Discussion: a. To what extent are Joshua 2:9,11,24 true for the Body of Christ?
b. In Luke 8:26-33, 10:17-20, who are the enemies of God and His people? Why are those enemies afraid?
c. Do you think our current demonic enemies are afraid of us? Why or why not?
d. What about human opponents of God and His people?

43

For Thought and Discussion: a. Why do you think God chose the family of a pagan prostitute to be the one family saved out of Jericho and to join the covenant people?

b. Why do you think He chose Rahab to be an ancestor of Christ?

For Thought and Discussion: According to John 17:15,18 and Ephesians 4:17-24, to what extent should a Christian make the kind of complete break with his past sinful life that Rahab made? Can you think of any other New Testament passages that show us how to act in this area?

10. What one truth from 2:1-24 stands out as something you want to take to heart this week?

11. How is this truth relevant to your life? How do you fall short or need to grow in this area?

12. What can you do to impress this truth on your heart and put it into practice?

13. List any questions you have about 2:1-24.

44

For the group

Warm-up. Ask everyone to think of one thing he or she has done recently to show that he or she has genuine faith in the Lord. If you find it hard to think of anything, make this a topic of prayer and discussion when you get to application.

Read aloud and summarize.

Questions. There is a lot of reading in this lesson because of the Study Skill and the historical background. Don't get bogged down in either of these. You can review the Study Skill periodically as you examine future episodes.

Focus on how Rahab showed faith in the Lord and how that affected what happened to her. Discuss both how her story is important to the overall message of Joshua and how it is relevant today. Encourage each person to choose one truth from the lesson to act on. Plan to share next week how this affected your lives during the week. This should not be a time to embarrass or impress each other, but a chance to encourage and help one another to apply what you learn.

Worship. Thank God for welcoming the Rahabs of the world into His people. Praise Him for proving that He is God in heaven and on earth, and for striking fear into His enemies' hearts. Ask Him for the courage to stake your lives on the conviction that He has the world under control.

1. Gordon Fee and Douglas Stuart, *How to Read the Bible for All Its Worth* (Grand Rapids, Michigan: Zondervan Corporation, 1982), pages 74-78.
2. Jensen, page 37.
3. Hamlin, page 17.
4. Hamlin, page xviii.
5. Hamlin, pages xvii-xix.
6. Jensen, page 60.
7. Woudstra, page 109.
8. *The NIV Study Bible,* page 293.
9. Woudstra, page 74.

Optional Application: a. In what ways is your past like and unlike Rahab's?

b. Why is it important to you that God welcomes people like Rahab?

c. Who are the Rahabs—the unbelievers with stained pasts—that you encounter? How open are you to welcoming them into the community of God's people?

Optional Application: How can you show your faith through costly action as Rahab did?

JOSHUA 3:1-4:24

Jordan Crossing

Israel has been waiting nearly a week for the order to move out. At last the spies have returned with good news (2:24). Joshua has been up perhaps all night making final arrangements so that "Early in the morning" (3:1) the march on Canaan can begin. "After three days" (3:2), the cavalcade halts at the edge of the gorge cut by the Jordan River.

The nearer, upper level is green and fertile. Below it stretches a belt of lifeless grey clay, and below that is thick jungle concealing wild animals (Jeremiah 12:5, 50:44). At the bottom, a thousand yards down, the river tumbles by.[1] During most of the year the Jordan is shallow enough to cross easily here, but in early April the winter rains and melting mountain snows have swollen it to a torrent (Joshua 3:15).[2] How will Joshua get this crowd of armed warriors, women, children, donkeys, sheep, and goats across this flood? Read 3:1-4:24.

1. Basically, what happens in 3:1-4:24?

_____

_____

_____

_____

_____

_____

47

_____

_____

_____

Ark of the covenant (3:3,6,8,11,14,17; 4:7,9,18).
"Ark" is an old English word for a wooden
chest. This one had a hinged lid and contained
the tablets on which the covenant laws were
written (Exodus 25:10-22). It also contained a
jar of manna, the miraculous food with which
God sustained Israel in the wilderness (Exodus
16:33-34). The ark was called "of the covenant"
or **of the Testimony** (4:16) because it represented the covenant relationship and contained
the testimony to that covenant. When Israel
was encamped, the ark resided in the Most Holy
Place in the tabernacle.

It was also called ***the ark of the LORD***
(Joshua 4:11) and ***the ark of the LORD your God***
(4:5) because it was His throne and symbolized
His presence in the midst of His people. The lid
was called the "atonement cover" (Exodus
25:17; "mercy seat" in KJV) to remind Israel that
this was the throne of grace and mercy where
the blood of the sacrifices atoned for the people's sins. The ark represented God's character:
the covenant laws and promises affirmed that
He would be morally holy and faithful to His
oaths; His mercy covered and completed His
justice.

Finally, it was called ***the ark of the***
LORD—the Lord of all the earth (3:13; compare
3:11) to remind Israel that their God did not
lose His power and authority when they crossed
into Canaan, nor was He interested only in
Israel.

_____

2. What part did the ark play in the Jordan crossing (3:3-4,6,8,13-17; 4:4-11,15-18)?

_____

_____

_____

_____

_____

_____

_____

3. In light of what the ark represented, why do you think it figured in the events in this way? What was God trying to say?

_____

_____

_____

_____

_____

_____

For Thought and Discussion: God did not overcome all of Israel's obstacles as easily and painlessly as at the Jordan. Why do you think He didn't? Why doesn't He overcome all of your obstacles so easily? (*Optional:* See Romans 5:3-5, James 1:2-5, 1 Peter 1:6-7.)

Levites (3:3). The job of the tribe of Levi was to take care of the tabernacle and its furnishings. Levites always carried the ark when Israel traveled (Numbers 3:5-31).

A thousand yards (3:4). The people had to stay two thousand cubits behind the ark in order to watch the route it took and to maintain space around the holy object. When the ark was just reaching the edge of the water, the line of Israelites would have just reached the upper edge of the gorge. None of the people began the steep descent until the awesome piling up of the waters was complete.

Consecrate yourselves (3:5). Israel did this before meeting God at Mount Sinai (Exodus 19:10,14-15), and now did it again in preparation for the "amazing things" the Lord would do at the Jordan. Consecration involved washing oneself and one's clothing, abstaining from sex for a certain period, and probably self-examination and repentance from sin.

For Thought and Discussion: How do we know that the Lord is among us since we have no tangible symbol like the ark? (See John 14:15-17, Ephesians 1:13-14.)

For Thought and Discussion: a. How was Jesus' experience at the Jordan a fulfillment of Israel's experience there (Matthew 3:13-17)?
b. What do you think is a Christian's Jordan crossing?

4. What were the purposes of the miracle at the Jordan?

3:7, 4:14 _____

_____

_____

3:9-11 _____

_____

_____

_____

4:24 _____

_____

_____

_____

5. How was the Jordan crossing like the Red Sea crossing of the previous generation (Exodus 14:18,21-22,29-31; 15:11-18)? How did it serve similar purposes?

_____

_____

_____

_____

_____

6. Future generations were told, "the LORD your God dried up the Jordan before *you* . . . he dried it [the Red Sea] up before *us*" (4:23). Those future generations were not present at the Red Sea or at the Jordan. Why do you suppose Israel spoke of "we" and "us"? (*Optional:* See Deuteronomy 5:3.)

_____

_____

_____

_____

_____

For Thought and Discussion: a. Stone monuments were often used for the purpose you wrote in question 7 (Joshua 24:26, 1 Samuel 7:12). In your judgment, why are physical monuments so useful for this?

b. Israel built one monument in the midst of the river, and one on the Canaan side. What do you think was the message of each monument? Have you ever experienced anything similar? If so, remember that experience.

This is how you will know (3:10). The Lord proved two crucial things by cutting off the Jordan waters:

1. "Who is the true and mighty God—the God of Israel or the god on whom the Canaanites depend (Baal, who was believed to reign as king among the gods because he had triumphed over the sea-god)? By opening the way through the flooded Jordan the Lord [showed] both Israel and the Canaanites that he is Lord over the waters (as he was at the 'Red Sea,' at the flood [of Noah] and at creation) and that he is able to establish his own order in the world."

2. "Who has the rightful claim to the land—the Lord or the Canaanites? . . . By passing safely through the Jordan at the head of his army the Lord showed the rightness of his claim on the land. In the ancient Near East a common way for obtaining the judicial verdict of the gods was by compelling the accused to submit to trial by water ordeal. Usually this involved casting him into a river (if the accused drowned, the gods had found him guilty; if not, the gods had declared him innocent). In Israel, however, another form of water ordeal was practiced (see Numbers 5:16-28). Significantly, the Lord [entered] the Jordan first and then remain[ed] there until his whole army had crossed safely over. Thus his claim to the land was vindicated before the eyes of all who heard about it. And it was his claim, not Israel's; she came through the Jordan only with him and as his army, 'baptized' to his service."[3]

7. What was the meaning of the twelve-stone monument set up at Gilgal (4:4-7,19-24)?

_____

_____

51

For Thought and Discussion: a. Why did God care what "all the peoples of the earth" thought of Him (4:24)? See 3:11,13.

b. Does He still care? If so, how should this affect what we do? (Consider John 17:20-23.) Meditate on this truth and its implications for you personally.

Optional Application: Do you know deep down what 3:10 and 4:24 say? Do you fear the Lord with your thoughts and actions? Meditate on these verses, and ask God to help you know these truths and fear Him. How would this affect the way you handle your current circumstances?

Cut off (3:13), *stand up in a heap* (3:13), *stopped flowing* (3:16), *dried up* (4:23). God has not seen fit to give us the specifics of this miracle, but it seems that the waters were blocked at Adam, about nineteen miles north of Jericho. The blockage may have been a massive and precisely timed landslide (in 1927 a landslide blocked this part of the Jordan for more than twenty hours).[4] Or, it may have been something even more supernatural.

Fear the LORD (4:24). "The most fundamental expression in the O[ld] T[estament] for faith or religion. That fear . . . is not slavish dread but rather contains an element of recognition of God's glory and majesty along with trust" (Psalm 130:4).[5] Rahab's fear led her to transfer her allegiance to the Lord (Joshua 2:9-13). She had more fear and respect for the Lord than for what her overlord might do to her. By contrast, the Canaanite kings' fear moved them to despair (5:1) and bravado (10:1-5).

8. What did the Jordan crossing teach Israel about its leadership?

52

Study Skill—Applying Old Testament Narratives

Keep the following five guidelines in mind when you try to apply Old Testament narratives to yourself:

1. What people do in narratives is not necessarily a good example for us. Frequently it is just the opposite. (Chapter 7 is an instance of this.)

2. Most of the characters in narratives are far from perfect, and so are their actions. (See chapters 7 and 9.) Thus, we should not try to copy everything even a great man like Joshua does. We should let the rest of Scripture, especially the New Testament, guide us in drawing lessons for application.

3. We are not always told at the end of a narrative whether what happened was good or bad. We are expected to be able to decide that on the basis of what God has said directly elsewhere in the Scriptures.

4. In every case, God is speaking to and dealing with a particular person. We should not think we are supposed to do everything He tells someone in the narrative to do. Since He commanded different tactics in almost every one of Israel's battles, we can't assume that we should adopt one or another of those tactics for one of our battles. Instead of looking for tactics to copy, we should focus on God's character, His aims, and the variety of His methods. We should pray for discernment from the Holy Spirit and uncoerced confirmation from other Christians before we apply a specific command (such as to march into the river or set an ambush) to ourselves.

5. If God's Word illustrates a principle that the New Testament would uphold, then we can apply the principle to *genuinely comparable* situations in our own lives. Our task is to discern the principle accurately and make sure that our situations are truly comparable. This is not always easy, so it always requires wisdom from the Holy Spirit and guidance from the New Testament. Discussion with other discerning Christians also helps guard against error.[6]

For Thought and Discussion: a. What are some of the things God has done in your life and the Church's life to teach you what the Jordan crossing was supposed to teach Israel (3:10, 4:24)? See, for example, Acts 1:8, Ephesians 1:19.

b. How was Israel supposed to respond to this revelation of God's power? How should you respond?

For Thought and Discussion: a. Why do you think it was necessary for God to exalt Joshua in the eyes of Israel?

b. Would this miracle have inclined Israel to revere Joshua at the Lord's expense? Why or why not? Why was this important?

Optional Application: The flooded Jordan was an "impossible" obstacle to entering the inheritance. What "impossible" obstacles are between you and the abundant, joyful life God wants you (or other people you know) to inherit? Talk with God about this, and ask Him to act mightily to overcome these obstacles. Make this a persistent prayer.

Optional Application: Israel faced a crisis at the Jordan: to hang back in the wilderness or to go on into dangerous but promised Canaan. Do you face a choice to cross the river or turn back? If so, ask God to give you courage and wisdom to go on in faith. Ask others to pray with you, if necessary.

9. What truth in 3:1-4:24 stands out as most significant to you right now?

_____

_____

_____

_____

10. How is this truth relevant to your life? How do you fall short or want to grow in this area?

_____

_____

_____

_____

_____

11. What concrete steps can you take to begin putting this truth into practice this week?

_____

_____

_____

_____

_____

12. If you have any questions about 3:1-4:24, write them down.

_____

_____

_____

_____

For the group

Warm-up. Try one of these questions:

> "What is the most serious trial or obstacle you are currently facing in your battle to spread God's Kingdom?"
>
> "How have you experienced God's power, by which He blocked the Jordan and raised Jesus from death?"

Read aloud. To make this more interesting, ask several people to read sections of 3:1-4:24.

Summarize. Have someone tell basically what happens in 3:1-4:24. If some members had difficulty following the story, explain that Hebrew narrative is often episodic rather than chronological. That is, the author tells all about one aspect of an event, then backtracks in time to tell about another aspect. Or, he summarizes a whole episode before giving the details step by step. Or, he adds details each time he tells about something (such as when Joshua gives the orders and then when the people carry them out). We who think chronologically sometimes have to think hard to figure out what happened.

Questions. Many Christian hymns use the Jordan crossing as a symbol of death, the crossing from this wilderness life into Heaven. However, the New Testament suggests that our Canaan is the Kingdom of God which is here and now as well as yet to come. The battles to possess the earth as God's realm take place now, both in the spiritual and the physical world. So, the Jordan crossing most naturally represents the decision to join God's people and their struggle to possess their inheritance. In the New Testament, this is being "baptized into Christ" (Romans 6:2-4) as Christ was baptized in the Jordan. (The decision does not always occur exactly when physical baptism occurs, but this is what baptism is supposed to signify.) You might discuss this symbolism in your group after you have discussed what the Jordan experience was meant to teach Israel. As the Study Skill on page 53 emphasizes, try to see how your situation is like and unlike Israel's. Try to grasp what God was saying to Israel then, as well as what He is saying to you now. As usual, encourage each member to make some specific application of what he or she has learned.

Summarize.

Worship. Sing some songs about the Jordan crossing, and think about what they mean to you. Also, use 3:10 and 4:24 to spark praise of God. Affirm that He is the Lord of all the earth, the Mighty One who deserves to be feared, the God who is present with His people, leading them through the waters into battle.

1. Hamlin, page 30; Woudstra, page 81.
2. *The NIV Study Bible*, page 295.
3. *The NIV Study Bible*, page 295.
4. *The NIV Study Bible*, page 295.
5. Woudstra, page 97.
6. Fee and Stuart, page 78.

JOSHUA 5:1-12

Final Preparations

The Lord has begun to fulfill His promises to Israel: He has not left the people to die in the wilderness but has led them safely into Canaan. The miraculous act of grace at the Jordan has shown that "the living God is among you and that he will certainly drive out before you the Canaanites . . ." (3:10) and "that the hand of the LORD is powerful . . ." (4:24).

It is still not time to attack the enemy, however. Militarily, the army is ready, but there are some final spiritual preparations to be made. Read 5:1-12.

Circumcision (5:1-9)

1. Recall the effect the Jordan crossing was supposed to have on the nations (4:24). How did it affect the Amorite and Canaanite kings (5:1)?

   _____

   _____

2. This gave Israel time to perform a rite that was insane from a military point of view—an operation that incapacitated most of the fighting men for several days. Read Genesis 17:1-14. What did circumcision signify for Israel?

   _____

   _____

57

_____

_____

_____

_____

_____

Flint knives (5:2). These probably show that the
ceremony dates back to a time before metal was
widely available. Also, modern researchers have
verified that flint makes a better, sharper surgi-
cal instrument than bronze or iron.[1]

Circumcise . . . again (5:2). The rite had not been
performed since Israel left Egypt. Everyone who
was over twenty years old when Israel refused to
enter Canaan was dead, except Joshua and
Caleb (Numbers 14:1-45). Therefore, there were
still men living who were between forty and
sixty; these were circumcised in Egypt but were
under twenty when the curse was laid on the
people. Every other male was uncircumcised, for
the accursed generation was not allowed to put
the mark of God's covenant favor on its children. Now it was like the time of Abraham all
over again, for every male over eight days old
was to be circumcised.

The reproach of Egypt (5:9). The reproach the
Egyptians would have cast upon Israel and God
if Israel had perished in the desert after escap-
ing from Egypt. The Egyptians would have
scoffed that God really wasn't powerful or faithful enough to keep His promises, or that Israel
was too paltry or defiled to keep His love
(Exodus 32:7-14, Numbers 14:13-16,
Deuteronomy 9:28).[2]

3. God refused to let anyone born in the wilderness be circumcised as long as the forty years of
wandering went on. In light of Genesis 17:1-14,
what was God saying about Israel by doing this?

_____

_____

58

_____

_____

_____

4. God commanded all Israel to be circumcised once the accursed generation had died and the people were safely in Canaan. How did this roll away the reproach of Egypt?

_____

_____

_____

_____

_____

5. a. Israel's circumcision was a cutting away of physical flesh. Among other meanings, it signified circumcision of the heart (Deuteronomy 10:16, 30:6), the cutting away of the stubborn callous that makes a heart unresponsive to God.

What "circumcision" do Christians experience as a sign of entering the new covenant (Colossians 2:11-15)?

_____

_____

_____

_____

_____

_____

b. What reproach does this roll away, and how? (Think of your own life and Israel's reproach. If you like, see Romans 3:10-18, Ephesians 2:11-13.)

_____

_____

Optional Application: a. Do you ever feel that God is either not loving or not powerful enough to save you from destruction? If so, why?

b. How has God rolled away this reproach that the Accuser whispers to you? Think of experiences in your own life and in biblical history. Look for passages of Scripture to memorize and meditate on this week (such as Romans 5:6-11; 8:1-4,31-39; Ephesians 2:1-7).

For Thought and Discussion: Only circumcised men and women belonging to their households could celebrate the Passover (Exodus 12:48-49). Why do you think the Lord required this? Consider the meaning of circumcision.

_____

_____

_____

_____

_____

Passover (5:10-12)

Israel crossed the Jordan and reached Gilgal on the tenth day of Abib, the first month of Israel's calendar (Joshua 4:19). On that day forty years earlier, Israel had selected the lambs for the first Passover in Egypt (Exodus 12:1-5). On the eleventh of Abib, Israel's men were circumcised and so brought into the fullness of the covenant relationship with God. On the twelfth and thirteenth, the men rested and healed (Joshua 5:8).

6. Describe what Israel did on the fourteenth of Abib (Joshua 5:10; Exodus 12:6-30,43-51).

_____

_____

_____

_____

_____

_____

_____

7. What was the Passover meant to teach Israel about the Lord and His relationship to Israel?

_____

_____

_____

_____

60

_____

_____

_____

_____

For Further Study:
a. For the spiritual implications of manna, see Deuteronomy 8:1-18, John 6:25-59, 2 Corinthians 8:15.
   b. How is Christ for us like both manna and the fruit of the promised land?

For Israel, the Passover sacrifice and meal pointed backward toward the redemption from Egypt and forward toward a full rest and redemption. When Jesus celebrated the Passover before His death, He demonstrated how His own body and blood would be the sacrifice of the new covenant (Luke 22:14-20). In His crucifixion, He became the true Passover lamb (1 Corinthians 5:7-8). Greek Christians call Easter *Pascha*, from *Pesach*, the Hebrew for Passover. Easter is the annual, and the Lord's Supper is the more frequent, Christian celebration of the true Passover. Both feasts point back to the redemption at Calvary and forward toward the banquet in the fulfilled Kingdom of God (Luke 22:15-16, Revelation 19:9). Like Israel, we celebrate in the midst of, and in preparation for, the battles of Canaan.

Manna (Joshua 5:12). God provided this food miraculously throughout the desert wandering (Exodus 16:13-36). It looked like flakes of frost or resin, and tasted like coriander (Exodus 16:14, Numbers 11:7). It nourished but was not very exciting fare.

8. Why was the ceasing of the manna significant for Israel (Joshua 5:12, Deuteronomy 8:2-10)?

_____

_____

_____

_____

_____

_____

For Thought and Discussion: a. Did God stop providing for Israel when the manna stopped? Why or why not?

b. Why is this important for us to remember?

c. How does God provide for you?

Optional Application: a. What does 5:1-12 teach you about God's nature and character?

b. How are these aspects of Him personally relevant to you? How do they make you want to respond in prayer and action?

9. Circumcision, the Passover, and eating from the land were Israel's final preparations before confronting the Canaanites. Summarize what these events should have taught and accomplished for the people.

_____

_____

_____

_____

_____

_____

10. What one insight from this lesson would you like to focus on this week?

_____

_____

_____

_____

_____

11. How would you like this truth to affect your life?

_____

_____

_____

_____

_____

12. What can you do to take this insight to heart so that it will affect your thoughts and actions?

_____

_____

For Further Study:
Joshua 1:1-5:12 is about how God prepared Israel to begin conquering Canaan. Make your own outline or list of this section, showing how each episode helped prepare Israel. (What necessary preparation took place in chapter 1? In chapter 2?)

13. List any questions you have about 5:1-12.

For the group

Warm-up. Ask the group what signs (evidence) God has given each of you that you have an intimate relationship with Him. Some people may think mainly of internal evidence like the awareness of God's presence during prayer. Others may think of historical evidence like Jesus' death and resurrection, or of personal experiences like baptism or deliverance from some affliction. Don't spend a lot of time analyzing each other's answers now. Come back to this question after you have looked at the signs God gave Israel: safe passage from the desert to Canaan, circumcision, the Passover, and the fruit of the land. Have you experienced evidence that parallels each of Israel's?

Read aloud and summarize.

Questions. You could structure your discussion like this:

1. *Circumcision*: What did it mean? Why was it significant that Israel performed the rite at this point? (Look back to chapters 1-4 and forward to chapters 6-11. How did circumcision help prepare Israel for its battles?) What does circumcision mean for Christians? How is our circumcision a necessary preparation for the battles to possess our inheritance?

2. *Passover*: What did it mean? Why was it significant at this point? How did it help Israel pre-

For Further Study:
Study all God's covenants in the Old Testament: with Noah and all the earth (Genesis 9:1-17); with Abraham (Genesis 12:1-3, 13:14-17, 15:1-21, 17:1-16); with Israel through Moses (Exodus 19:3-20:21); with David and his successors (2 Samuel 7:8-16; Psalm 89:3-4,19-37); with the Levites (Numbers 25:10-13, Malachi 2:4-5); the new covenant foretold (Jeremiah 31:31-34). What do these reveal about God and His plans?

pare? What are our Passover celebrations? How are they necessary repeated preparations for our battles?

3. *Grain instead of manna*: What did this mean? Why was it a necessary change? (We haven't made a point of Christian parallels, because they are not as simple as circumcision and Passover. Christ compares Himself to manna in John 6, but we also enjoy some of the fruits of the Kingdom as we battle. It is dangerous to push for wooden parallelism and symbolism between Old Testament narratives and the Christian life. The symbols are fluid and overlap.) What does the change from manna to grain show about the ways God provides for His people?

4. What should these events have taught Israel about God? What have you learned about Him?

5. How is all this personally relevant to each of you? How will you respond?

Summarize and wrap up.

Worship. Thank God for giving Israel signs to guarantee the covenant relationship. Thank Him for the signs of your relationship with Him. Thank Him for removing your reproach and demonstrating by His daily care that He loves you.

Covenants

Both circumcision and Passover were signs of God's *covenant* with Israel. Although this word rarely appears in Joshua (3:6, 7:11, 9:6, 24:25), the idea pervades the book. A covenant in ancient times was simply a treaty, pact, or contract between political allies, friends, business partners, etc. A sovereign would make a covenant with a vassal (a *vassal* was the leader of a subject clan or tribe; he made treaties on behalf of his people).[3] The overlord agreed to protect and justly rule the vassal people, and they agreed to serve and obey him. Friends could make covenants to be loyal to each other as brothers. Marriage was a covenant between two individuals and two families. The covenant between God and Israel had all of these elements: Israel was God's vassal, His bride, and His friend.

---

1. Woudstra, page 99; *The NIV Study Bible*, page 297.

2. *The NIV Study Bible*, page 297; Woudstra, page 102.
3. Technically, the covenant was a personal pact between the sovereign and the leader of the subject group, but the leader was acting for the group.

JOSHUA 5:13-6:27

Jericho

The Israelite army is ready to fight its first battle in Canaan, and Joshua is ready to lead it. He may be expecting a conventional siege, but this opening venture will be a bit different from future ones. The Lord has another lesson to teach. Read 5:13-6:27.

Orders received (5:13-6:5)

1. Joshua goes "near Jericho" perhaps to scout his quarry one last time before the attack. From his question in 5:13, what does he apparently think when he sees the man standing with a drawn sword?

   _____

   _____

   _____

   _____

2. The man says he is neither for Israel nor for her enemies (5:14). Why is this an important lesson for Joshua?

   _____

   _____

   _____

For Thought and Discussion: Why was the ground holy where Joshua was standing? (For some possible reasons, see Exodus 3:1-10, Leviticus 25:23, Joshua 1:6.)

For Thought and Discussion: Why do you think the Lord said, "I have delivered Jericho . . ." (6:2) instead of "I will deliver . . ."?

_____

_____

Commander of the army of the LORD (5:14). Scripture sometimes portrays the Lord's army, or "host," as being composed of angels (1 Kings 22:19, Psalm 103:20-21). The word translated "commander" is used of princes, royal officials, and military captains (Genesis 12:15, 21:22; Numbers 22:13). In Daniel 10:13,20-21; 12:1 this word apparently refers to angels of high authority in God's army.[1] Some people think the commander in Joshua is one such angel, while others think he is Christ appearing before His Incarnation.

    My Lord (5:14) was a term of respect for a superior. Joshua was not necessarily calling the commander God.[2] A man might fall on the ground in **reverence** (or "worship") to an angel who represented God, since "worship paid to him [God's representative] is paid to Yahweh himself."[3] In the ancient Near East, a king's ambassador was regarded as an extension of the king and treated like the king himself. So, we cannot decide conclusively whether this was Christ or an angel.

_____

3. The commander said, "I have now come" (5:14). What had he come to do?

_____

_____

_____

_____

_____

The LORD said (6:2). Whether or not the commander was Christ, he was the Lord's representative and spoke in His name. It appears that the commander spoke the orders from the Lord in 6:2-5.

Optional Application: Who is in charge of your life's battles? Who gives the orders, and who obeys? Pray about this, and ask God to help you change if necessary. Concentrate on this issue this week.

4. Joshua asked what message the commander had for him (5:14). What was the commander's message from the Lord (5:15, 6:2-5)?

_____

_____

_____

_____

_____

_____

_____

Optional Application: Do you expect God to be on your side, or are you doing all you can to be on His side (5:13-14)? How can you grow in this area?

5. What do you think this encounter with the commander of the Lord's army was meant to teach Joshua?

_____

_____

_____

_____

_____

_____

Orders obeyed (6:6-27)

"Colorful and spectacular" is how Irving Jensen describes the drama at Jericho.[4] The sights: seven robed priests proceeding with trumpets around a seemingly impenetrable brick fortress; Levites following with the ark; an honor guard marching before and after the priests and ark; thousands of Israelites in battle array. The sounds: silence for seven days except for the chill, piercing blasts on

69

the trumpets; a final great blast and a shout of triumph from every throat; the crash of walls collapsing; bedlam as the Israelite army pours into the city.

Since Jericho was less than seven hundred yards around, the head of the procession was back at camp in Gilgal each day by the time the last marchers were reaching the city. On the last day, the warriors stayed and ringed the city for the attack.

In biblical symbolism, seven represents perfection and completeness (see, for example, Genesis 1:1-2:3; 4:24; 7:2; Leviticus 4:6,17; 8:11; Proverbs 24:16; Matthew 18:21; and the fifty-four sevens in Revelation). The reason seems to be that God created the world in seven days. The significance of destroying Jericho on the seventh day (was it a Sabbath on which work was normally forbidden?) is worth pondering.

The sound of trumpets was a call to arms for the Israelites, a warning to the doomed people of Jericho, and a herald of the Holy God just as He came at Mount Sinai (Exodus 19:13-19; 2 Samuel 6:15; Amos 3:6; Revelation 8:6-9:21, 11:15-19). It was a sound of war and of the coming of God's Kingdom—the ram's horn was blown annually to proclaim the civil New Year (Numbers 10:9-10, 29:1-6). Every fiftieth year (seven times seven, plus one), the trumpet announced the Year of Jubilee, the year of liberation and justice (Leviticus 25:8-55).[5]

The shout was a battle cry to encourage friends and terrorize foes. It was also a victory cry and a sound of joy when God came to fight for His people against the fortresses of wickedness.[6]

Jericho was the accursed city, the first representative of Canaan's evil. It was a stronghold of idolatry, immorality, violence, and exploitation of the poor. Its destruction was a sentence decreed by the Just and Holy God.

6. In the procession across the Jordan, the ark of the Lord led. What might be the significance of the ark being in the midst of the army (6:9)?

_____

_____

_____

_____

_____

7. Most of Canaan was taken through ordinary military means. Why do you think the Lord chose to give Israel Jericho in this miraculous way?

_____

_____

_____

_____

_____

For Further Study:
a. Using a concordance, trace the theme of doomed cities through Scripture: Cain's city, Nimrod's city, Babel, Sodom, Nineveh (Nahum 3:1), Tyre (Ezekiel 26:17-19), Jerusalem (Jeremiah 20-39), Babylon (Isaiah 13:19-20, 47:10-11; Revelation 18:10). What do these cities represent, and why does God destroy them?
b. What kind of city does God intend for His people (Revelation 21:1-22:5)?

Devoted (6:17). The Hebrew word *herem* is translated "completely destroyed" (2:10), "devoted things" (6:18), "destruction" (6:18), "devoted" (6:21), and "destroyed" (6:21). Something or someone *herem* "was absolutely and irrevocably consecrated so that it could not be redeemed"[7] (Leviticus 27:28-29). It belonged to the Lord, and He could do with it whatever He chose. The idea often was that the thing or person was devoted to utter destruction. *Herem* was serious because it reflected God's radical holiness.

The Lord had laid all Canaan under this curse, but He allowed a milder form in some cases (Deuteronomy 20:10-18; Joshua 8:2, 11:12-14). Jericho received the strictest form. Canaan's *herem* foreshadowed the judgment "God will mete out to those whose unrighteousness will be full (compare Genesis 15:16) in the end of days (see Jeremiah 51:63-64, Revelation 18:19-21)."[8]

8. How was the *herem* curse applied to Jericho (6:17-26)?

_____

_____

_____

For Thought and Discussion: Rahab's family was saved from the curse. Why? What does this reveal about God?

For Thought and Discussion: Israel's conquests have been used to justify wars of conquest in recent centuries. Christians and Jews have said that God promised them a piece of land and told them to wipe out the natives. How would you verify or disprove such a claim? Do Joshua and the rest of Scripture justify that application? Why or why not?

_____

_____

9. Why do you suppose God applied the curse with the utmost strictness to Jericho?

_____

_____

_____

_____

_____

_____

10. What do you learn about God from the way Jericho was conquered and destroyed?

_____

_____

_____

_____

_____

_____

_____

_____

11. What one insight from 5:13-6:27 seems most relevant to you?

_____

_____

_____

_____

_____

12. How would you like this truth to affect your life and your character?

_____

_____

_____

_____

_____

13. What steps can you take to begin making this happen, by God's grace?

_____

_____

_____

_____

_____

_____

14. List any questions you have about 5:13-6:27.

_____

_____

_____

_____

For the group

Warm-up. Ask everyone to think about this question: "Do you want God to be on your side in the battles of your life?" Give everyone a chance to answer this silently to himself or herself. Then ask, "Is this a good or a flawed attitude? Why?"

Read aloud and summarize.

Questions. Don't be distracted by debating the identity of the commander of the Lord's army. God has not seen fit to make this explicit, and the primary point of the story is the same either way.

Again, don't be sidetracked into deciding whether the mass killing of men, women, children, and animals was a loving thing for God to command. This episode is meant to stress God's holy hatred of wickedness and His power and will to eradicate it. The Creator has a right to destroy rebels, and the animals are His, too (Deuteronomy 7:1-11, 9:1-6, 32:39-43; Psalm 50:10-12). Rather than criticizing His justice, we should remember that were it not for His love and mercy, we would all be under the curse. Like Romans 1:18-3:20, the *herem* should impress on us how amazing God's grace is in light of His holiness. The fate of Jericho, Sodom, and Babylon should motivate us to purify ourselves, as He is pure (1 John 3:3-10).

The box at the end of lesson nine may help you if you decide to discuss whether Joshua justifies military conquests for Christians. You should also use the New Testament to guide you. What is our inheritance? How do we fight for it? Was military conquest a unique stage in God's plan of redemption, or is it a norm that He sometimes repeats? How do you know?

The main thrust of this lesson is, what was God trying to teach Israel through the events of 5:13-6:27? Then second, what is He trying to teach us? How is our situation similar and different? What should each of you do about what you have learned?

Summarize.

Worship. Praise the Lord of Hosts—the Commander in Chief of the hosts of heaven and His people on earth. Praise Him for giving Jericho into Israel's hands by His power alone. Praise Him for His utter holiness that makes the land He touches holy and requires all that is unholy to be destroyed. Ask Him to completely cleanse your life of unholiness and to fight His battles in your life. Ask Him to be your commander and to help you take His holiness and authority seriously.

1. Woudstra, page 105.
2. *The NIV Study Bible*, page 297; Woudstra, page 105.
3. J. A. Soggin, *Joshua* (Philadelphia: Fortress Press, 1972), page 78; see also Woudstra, page 105, note 4.
4. Jensen, page 58.

5. Hamlin, pages 50-51.
6. Hamlin, pages 51-52.
7. Woudstra, page 113.
8. Woudstra, page 113.

JOSHUA 7:1-26

Trouble Valley

The Lord gave Jericho into Israel's hands by a sovereign act of power, His pledge that He would continue to lead the conquest. The response He demanded was absolute loyalty and obedience from His soldiers. This was His war, to be played by His rules.

One standing order was that everyone and everything in Jericho was *herem*—devoted to the Lord. All but the metals was to be destroyed; the metals were assigned to the Lord's treasury (6:19). Joshua had stressed this command (6:17-19), and as far as he and most of his army knew, everyone had obeyed. But read 7:1-26.

1. What did Achan son of Carmi do (7:1,20-21)?

_____

_____

_____

_____

_____

2. How did the Lord react to this action (7:1,4-5,12)?

_____

_____

a. What happened to the many descendants of Adam when that one man sinned (Romans 5:12,15,17)? Why?

b. What happens to "the many" who have faith because one of their kinsmen—Jesus—performed one right-eous act (Romans 5:15-18)?

c. What does this principle of "one kinsman for many" tell you about God's system?

3. How did He view Achan's deed (7:1,11-12)?

4. God says, "*Israel* has sinned; *they* have violated my covenant . . . *they* have stolen, *they* have lied . . . *they* have been made liable to destruc-tion [made *herem*]" (7:11-12). Many died because of one man's sin (22:20). Why do you think God held all Israel responsible for one man's deed?

5. Do you observe the same principle in operation among Christians to any extent? If so, why and in what ways? If not, why not? (See, for exam-ple, 1 Corinthians 12:26.)

Tore his clothes . . . sprinkled dust on their heads (7:6). Both were signs of great distress or grief.

6. In his anguish at being defeated by Ai, Joshua asked the Lord three questions and made two statements. What were they (7:7-9)?

question _____

_____

_____

statement _____

_____

_____

question _____

_____

_____

statement _____

_____

_____

question _____

_____

For Thought and Discussion: a. How did Joshua err in 7:2-4? What did he neglect to do?

b. Do you ever neglect to do this in similar situations? Talk with God about this.

For Further Study: In considering how Joshua 7 might apply to Christian groups, consider 1 Corinthians 5:1-13, 2 Corinthians 2:5-11, Galatians 6:1-10, and James 5:16-20.

Sovereign LORD (7:7). "Lord GOD" in RSV and NASB. This title stresses God's lordship over events and over Israel.

Our name . . . your own great name (7:9). By an extraordinary act of magnanimity, the Lord had linked His own name—His own reputation and character—with Israel's. Like a marriage or an adoption, the covenant joined their names, so that "Yahweh" became "the God of Israel." If the Lord wiped out Israel, His name would be stained (Numbers 14:13-16; Ezekiel 20:9,14,22).

79

For Thought and Discussion: Why do you suppose it was necessary for each Israelite to consecrate himself before the lots were cast (7:13)?

For Further Study: Does the story of Achan contradict the principle God lays down in Ezekiel 18:20? Why or why not?

For Thought and Discussion: First John 1:8-2:2 says that Jesus' blood atones for our sins if we confess them. By contrast, an animal sacrifice could not atone for Achan, even after his confession. Galatians 6:7 says that a person reaps what he or she sows. If a Christian steals from God and confesses, do you believe that God forgives him without punishment (assuming he restores what was taken)? Why or why not?

7. What do you think of Joshua's words in 7:7-9? In light of what he knew, was he being reasonable or foolish? Why?

_____

_____

_____

_____

_____

_____

In response to Joshua's pleas, the Lord curtly ordered him to his feet, revealed the breach of covenant, and stated His terms for removing the curse from Israel (7:10-15).

8. Achan sinned, and all Israel lost in battle. One man broke the law, and the whole nation was under the curse. How was Israel permitted to cleanse itself (7:13-15)?

_____

_____

_____

_____

_____

_____

9. How does this balance the idea of collective responsibility?

_____

_____

_____

_____

_____

The tribe that the LORD takes (7:14). The precise way is not mentioned. The Urim and Thummim (Numbers 27:21, Deuteronomy 33:8) may have been used. Casting lots was a familiar way of seeking God's will, since God was thought to guide the lots (Proverbs 16:33, Acts 1:26).

Destroyed by fire (7:15). If a person sinned unintentionally, the Law provided a way for atonement: an animal could be sacrificed to pay the death penalty for sin. However, arrogant sins were considered blasphemy and so were punished severely (Numbers 15:27-31). Only one's own death could atone for these. God was serious about sin and *herem*.

A disgraceful thing (7:15). Elsewhere in the Old Testament, this Hebrew phrase is used only of sexual sins (Genesis 34:7, Deuteronomy 22:21, 2 Samuel 13:12). Achan had prostituted himself with the gods of Canaan, especially with lust for wealth, and so had committed adultery against his covenant Lord. Violating the covenant was equivalent to breaking marriage vows.

10. Why does honest confession "give glory to the LORD" (7:19)?

_____

_____

_____

_____

_____

Sinned against the LORD (7:20). Achan's (and Israel's) understanding of sin was different from that of other Near Eastern peoples. "In Egypt, for example, evil was not viewed as a rebellion against the divine will but merely as an aberration from the cosmic order. As such, sin was only evidence of ignorance on the part of the sinner. Contrition is, therefore, not found among the Egyptians."[1]

For Thought and Discussion: Why was the Lord so angry about the breaking of *herem* (7:11,15)? Why was this law so important to Him, and what does this reveal about His values?

For Thought and Discussion: What attitude does Joshua show toward the sinner who has cost lives, time, and shame (7:19)? Is this an example for Christian leaders? If so, how?

For Thought and Discussion: Achan's sin required public confession because it hurt the whole community. Is this ever true today? If so, when? If not, why not?

For Thought and Discussion: How does your culture view sin? Is it rebellion against God? Against society? Is it ignorance of the way the world works? Is it a sickness, a psychological flaw, or just being different? Does your society believe in sin at all?

For Further Study:
Compare the progression of Achan's sin (Joshua 7:21) to that of Eve (Genesis 3:6) and to James 1:13-15. Have you ever experienced this? How is it possible to resist this kind of temptation before it overwhelms us?

For Further Study:
Compare Joshua 7:1-26 to Acts 5:1-11. What similarities and differences do you observe? Why do you think the Lord was so drastic in dealing with these sinners? Why do you suppose He rarely does this kind of thing today?

His sons and daughters (7:24). Achan's whole family and all its possessions were made *herem* for his sin. On the one hand, God punishes "the children for the sins of the fathers to the third and fourth generation of those who hate me" (Deuteronomy 5:9). On the other hand, "Fathers shall not be put to death for their children, nor children put to death for their fathers; each is to die for his own sin" (Deuteronomy 24:16). Perhaps Achan's family cooperated in hiding the stolen goods, which were in the family tent, or perhaps God knew that the disease in Achan's character had infected his whole family. In any case, God judged that the children shared their father's guilt. God's Law held corporate guilt and individual responsibility in balance and tension.

Trouble . . . Achor (7:25-26). Achor means "disaster" or "trouble." Joshua made a rueful pun on Achan's name, and the name "Trouble Valley" stuck to the site. (Achan is called "Achar" in 1 Chronicles 2:7.)

11. What do you think Israel was supposed to learn from the severe consequences—both for the nation and for the thief's family—of Achan's sin?

_____

_____

_____

_____

_____

_____

12. How is the story of Achan relevant to us as Christians?

_____

_____

_____

_____

_____

13. What one truth from this chapter would you like to concentrate on this week for application?

_____

_____

_____

_____

14. How do you want this truth to affect you?

_____

_____

_____

_____

_____

15. What can you do to cooperate with God in accomplishing this?

_____

_____

_____

_____

_____

_____

16. List any questions you have about chapter 7.

_____

_____

_____

_____

For Thought and Discussion: a. In your judgment, do the private sins of individuals affect their families, churches, or fellowships? What evidence can you offer to support your view?

b. How should this affect the way we deal with our own temptations and sin, and those of others?

Optional Application: Ask the Lord if any sin of yours or of another person is preventing victory in your battles to further His Kingdom. Spend some time in prayer searching your heart and seeking God's guidance.

**Optional
Application:** Should
your church or fellow-
ship take an active
interest in encourag-
ing members to
repent of their sins, or
are sins a private
matter? What New
Testament teaching
can you cite to sup-
port your view? If you
think groups should
be concerned with
this, how do you
believe yours should
go about it? How can
you avoid judgmental-
ism, suspicion, and
meddling?

For the group

Warm-up. Ask the group, "Do you think it is possible to commit a sin that affects no one but yourself? If so, name one such sin." Save any discussion
of reasons why or why not until after you have
examined the story of Achan. Your ultimate conclu-
sions will depend partly on your own experience and
partly on the way you interpret Joshua 7 and
1 Corinthians 12.

Read aloud. To help the group feel the drama, you
can assign the roles of Joshua, Achan, the Lord, and
the narrator to different readers.

Summarize.

Questions. You may have to wrestle with the idea of
collective solidarity, since it is the opposite of the
individualism American culture teaches. (Many
other modern cultures take corporateness for
granted and think individualism is strange.) Why
did God hold first all Israel, then Achan's family, ac-
countable for his sin? Second, to what extent does
this apply to us in the New Testament era? To what
extent does God treat us as individuals, and to what
extent does He treat us as families, as groups, or as
one Body? Does 1 Corinthians 12 suggest that as
members of one Body we are affected by and held
responsible for what other believers do? Why or why
not? Have you observed the principle of corporateness ("body-ness") in Christian groups? Is the idea
of unity in Christ, which the New Testament
stresses, connected to the idea of corporate responsibility? If so, how? These are all questions you may
choose to tackle.

Collective accountability is connected to the
idea of covenant. Achan's sin was so serious because
it violated the covenant relationship God had with
Israel. God was covenanted with the whole people
and with each individual. The relationship with the
whole was broken until the violation was atoned for
by the individual responsible. Help the group to
grasp the balance between individual and group in
this story.

Your applications will depend in part on
whether you think corporate responsibility applies
to the Body of Christ. If you think it does, you may
want to examine yourselves to see how

84

your actions are affecting the battles you are fighting alongside other believers. If you think it doesn't, you may want to focus on God's holiness and His abhorrence of sin in this chapter. How are these relevant to each of you? How do they motivate you to deal with your own lives?

Worship. Don't let this meeting end on a heavy note. Praise the Holy One of Israel. If it is appropriate, confess your unfaithfulness silently or aloud, and so give glory to the Holy One. Thank Him for providing Jesus as atonement for your sins, to purge you and your community as Israel was purged by the utter destruction of Achan and his household.

1. Woudstra, page 129; citing *Documents from Old Testament Times*, edited by D. W. Thomas (New York, 1961), page 151.

JOSHUA 8:1-35

Covenant Restored

Israel now has one blazing victory and one embarrassing defeat to its credit. Ai controls the high point of the road from Jericho into the arteries of Canaan, so the city must be taken. Although Achan is dead, Joshua won't sleep easily until he knows Israel is in the Lord's good graces again. This battle will tell.

Read 8:1-35.

Ai (8:1-29)

1. What do the Lord's words in 8:1-2 signify, in light of chapter 7?

_____

_____

_____

_____

_____

2. What role does each of the following play in taking Ai?

the Lord (8:1-2,7-8,18-19) _____

_____

_____

For Thought and Discussion: This time, who gives the orders regarding the attack on Ai (8:1-2)? Why is this important?

For Thought and Discussion: When Joshua was acting on his own, he sent only a few soldiers to attack Ai (7:3-4). Is it significant that the Lord tells him to send "the whole army" (8:1,3)? Why do you think God places such emphasis on unity in the book of Joshua (1:12-18, 3:1, 4:1, 5:8, 6:3, 7:1)?

Optional Application: Who gives the orders in your life? How does this affect your defeat or victory? Review the past few weeks.

Optional Application: Do confession and cleansing restore your relationship to God as they did in Israel's case (7:26-8:1)? Why or why not? Consider taking time for this.

Joshua (8:3-13,15,18,26,28-29) _____

"all Israel" (8:3-13,15,19,21-27) _____

Hung the king (8:29). The Israelites did not execute criminals by hanging them from ropes. They did, however, impale them on trees or poles (the Hebrew word translated ***tree*** can mean either) after execution as an example to onlookers. (See Deuteronomy 21:22-23.)[1]

---

3. The author of the book of Joshua gives detailed descriptions of only a few of the dozens of battles Israel fought. In your judgment, why is the conquest of Ai important enough to recount in detail? (What does it contribute to the overall

88

message of Joshua? What should later generations of Israelites have learned from this story?)

_____

_____

_____

_____

_____

_____

_____

Covenant renewal (8:30-35)

4. In his farewell address to Israel, Moses instructed the nation to perform a ceremony at Mounts Gerizim and Ebal (see the map on page 9). What did Moses tell Israel to do?

Deuteronomy 27:1-4,8 (compare Joshua 8:32)

_____

_____

_____

_____

_____

Deuteronomy 27:5-7 (compare Joshua 8:30-31)

_____

_____

_____

_____

Deuteronomy 27:11-26 (compare Joshua 8:33)

_____

_____

Optional Application: Thank God for giving you victories in your battles to possess your inheritance and oust the enemies of the Kingdom. Ask God for your current orders, and spend some time listening daily this week. Just sit in silence with God, first meditating on Joshua 8 and then listening. What are God's orders for you as an individual, and what are His orders for your church in building His Kingdom?

For Thought and Discussion: Why do you think God allows His soldiers to take plunder from Ai (8:2) after the incident with Achan? What is the lesson here?

_____

_____

_____

5. What else did Joshua do besides what Moses
had said (Joshua 8:34-35)?

_____

_____

_____

_____

_____

Uncut stones (8:31). Exodus 20:25 required that
stone altars be made of uncut stones. Cutting
tools would "defile" an altar—perhaps because
using cut stones was a Canaanite practice, or
perhaps because stonecutting was for "idols,"
which the Second Commandment forbade
(Exodus 20:4-6; see also Exodus 20:22-26).[2]

Burnt offerings . . . fellowship offerings (8:31).
These same sacrifices were offered when Israel
first received the Law at Mount Sinai (Exodus
20:24). The Mount Ebal event was a renewal
and reminder of the covenant made at Sinai.

    Burnt offerings were given wholly to God
through fire. They were "atonement for unin-
tentional sin in general" and an "expression of
devotion, commitment and complete surrender
to God."[3] Fellowship offerings included a com-
munal meal with the sacrifice. They expressed
the relationship of peace and wholeness with
God and fellow Israelites that the atonement
sacrifice restored. They were acts of thanksgiv-
ing and joy.[4]

Copied on stones the law of Moses (8:32). The
stones were plastered so that the writing was
easy to read (Deuteronomy 27:2-4). We don't
know how much of the Law was copied—the
Ten Commandments? The blessings and curses
of Deuteronomy 28? All the laws of Deuteron-

90

omy? We do know that the ancients could get a fair amount of writing onto a stone monument.

A Jewish legend "claims that the law was written in seventy languages so that all the peoples of the earth might read . . . While the story is apocryphal, the sentiment it expresses of the worldwide claims of God's Torah is not."[5] God posted His Law in the very center of Canaan, like a king posting his decrees for the inhabitants of a newly claimed land.

All Israel . . . were standing (8:33). From Deuteronomy 27, it seems that six of the tribes stood on and around Mount Gerizim and six stood on and around Ebal. The Levites stood in between, with the ark in their midst. They read the blessings of covenant-keeping, and the people responded, "Amen." Then they read the curses of covenant-breaking, and the people answered, "Amen."

Shechem is a natural amphitheater. Mount Ebal is about a thousand feet above the valley floor, and Gerizim about eight hundred feet above. They "are about a mile and a half apart at the top but only about five hundred yards apart at the bottom."[6] If one stands on the top or sides of either mountain, one can hear anything said in a loud voice from the other mountain or the valley. It was an ideal site for a ceremony like this. In addition, from the top of either mountain one can survey most of the promised land.

6. The conquest of Ai may have given Israel its first opportunity to penetrate all the way to Shechem. Why do you think this was an appropriate time to reaffirm Israel's commitment to the Lord and His covenant?

_____

_____

_____

_____

_____

For Thought and Discussion: Do you know of any Christian ceremonies to re-affirm commitment to the Lord and His commands? Describe one, or look into the practices of other Christian groups. What purposes do such ceremonies have?

7. What might have been the purposes of . . .

posting a copy of God's covenant Law on a hill in the center of Canaan?

_____

_____

_____

_____

_____

offering burnt and fellowship offerings to the Lord?

_____

_____

_____

_____

_____

reading God's Law aloud to Israel?

_____

_____

_____

_____

reading aloud the blessings for obedience and the curses for disobedience to the covenant, and having all the people say "Amen" to them?

_____

_____

_____

_____

8. What important truths do you think Christians should learn from the accounts of the conquest of Ai and the covenant renewal at Ebal? How are these stories relevant to us?

_____

_____

_____

_____

_____

_____

9. What one truth from this chapter would you like to begin applying to your own life this week?

_____

_____

_____

_____

_____

10. How do you need to grow in this area, or how do you want this insight to affect you?

_____

_____

_____

_____

_____

11. What do you plan to do to make this more a part of your life?

_____

_____

_____

_____

_____

_____

12. List any questions you have about 8:1-35.

_____

_____

_____

_____

For the group

Warm-up. Ask, "When you have sinned, do you usually feel close to God again soon after confessing? Or
do you often continue to feel distant and ashamed
for a while? Why?" This question will help you get
to know each other a bit more deeply, and it will
also lead into chapter 8. The victory at Ai was God's
guarantee that confession and cleansing had restored fellowship, so there was no more need for
discomfort.

Questions. The military details of the conquest of Ai
are not all clear; see the commentaries if you are
interested. The point of the story is clear, so we
haven't dealt much with the details.

The covenant renewal ceremony may be a little
harder for group members to grasp, unless they
celebrate renewal ceremonies themselves. (For
instance, some churches have the congregation
renew their baptismal vows each time a new person
is baptized, or at Easter or another annual occa-
sion.) To follow what happened at the ceremony at
Ebal, you have to piece together Deuteronomy 27
and Joshua 8. Ask someone to explain step by step
what he thinks happened. Let the rest of the group
offer corrections or fill in missing details. Look at a
commentary on Deuteronomy or Joshua if you are
seriously confused. When you have a reasonable
grip on what happened, discuss the meaning of each
thing done. What did God want to impress on Israel
by each aspect of the ceremony? Then, why are each

of these things important for Christians to remember?

Worship. Thank God for keeping His promises to Israel again once fellowship was restored. Thank Him for the Law that guided Israel in living out that covenant relationship. Thank Him for your relationship with Him and for giving you His orders for victory over your spiritual enemies.

1. *The NIV Study Bible*, page 302.
2. Woudstra, page 147.
3. *The NIV Study Bible*, page 150.
4. *The NIV Study Bible*, page 150; Woudstra, page 147.
5. Woudstra, page 144, note 2.
6. Shaeffer, page 120.

JOSHUA 9:1-27

Gibeon's Deception

When the Lord dried up the Jordan to let Israel cross, the kings of Canaan were struck numb with fear (5:1). Then first Jericho and next Ai fell to the invaders, and Israel had gained the high ridge overlooking the whole land. The lords of the cities just south of Ai had to quell their panic or go down without a fight like Jericho. What could they do? Read 9:1-27 for the solution one group chose.

1. How did the kings of Canaan react to the news of Jericho and Ai (9:1-2)?

_____

_____

_____

_____

Hill country . . . western foothills . . . coast of the Great Sea . . . Lebanon (9:1). The author has most or all of Canaan in mind: the central mountain region from above Shechem to below Hebron; the lower rocky plateau west of the mountains; and the still lower seacoast further west.

Six of the seven peoples of Canaan from 3:10 are named. For their exact identifications, see the commentaries.

Treaty (9:6). This is the same word as "covenant" in 7:11 and 24:25. Just as Israel had a treaty or covenant with the Lord, so Gibeon wanted a treaty by which Gibeon would be the vassal and Israel would be the sovereign. People of the ancient Near East took covenants extremely seriously. Israel was the only nation known to have a treaty with a god, but treaties with men were always sworn in the names of gods.

2. The Gibeonites figured out that Israel intended to annihilate all the natives of Canaan. How did Gibeon hope to escape destruction (9:3-13)?

_____

_____

_____

_____

_____

_____

3. Why did Gibeon's ruse work (9:14-15)?

_____

_____

_____

_____

_____

Elders (9:11). There is no mention of a king of Gibeon. "Apparently the Gibeonite political administration differed from that of other cities of Canaan. . . ."[1] One reason why Gibeon preferred to ally with Israel rather than with its neighbors may have been that the Gibeonites did not care for the way the kings ruled their subjects. The elders of Israel might be more congenial masters than the oppressive Canaanite kings.

Assembly (9:15,18). All the men of fighting age probably had a say in the affairs of their clans and tribes. They apparently chose leaders from each tribe to represent them in some sort of republican committee called "the leaders of the assembly." This political system was very different from the tight, authoritarian class systems that prevailed in Egypt and Canaan.

For Thought and Discussion: Why do you think the Lord didn't just override Israel's treaty and command that it be broken?

4. Why were Joshua and the leaders wrong to make a peace treaty with Gibeon? (See Deuteronomy 7:1-6, 20:10-18.)

_____

_____

_____

_____

_____

5. What would have happened if Israel had broken an oath sworn in the Lord's name (Joshua 9:19-20)?

_____

_____

_____

_____

_____

6. a. Why do you suppose this would have happened, even though the Lord had forbidden such treaties?

_____

_____

_____

_____

_____

For Thought and Discussion: Israel's oath was apparently binding even though God did not approve what was sworn (9:19). Do you think this applies to Christians promising things God does not approve of? Why or why not? Support your view with Scripture.

b. What does this tell you about God's nature and the way He regards the use of His name?

_____

_____

_____

_____

We cannot touch them (9:19). When David was king in Israel, he learned that the cause of a three-year famine was that Saul had killed many Gibeonites in his misplaced zeal for the Lord. The famine was the Lord's punishment for breaking the oath made centuries before by Israel's leaders (2 Samuel 21:1-9).

Woodcutters and water carriers (9:21,23,27). A large nation like Israel used a lot of wood and water. The daily offerings at the tabernacle required huge amounts for burning and cleaning up. The Gibeonites' status was better than being dead, but they were still cursed to be menial servants ("slaves" in NASB and RSV), less than full members of the covenant community. However, they were in the Lord's service. Their city was assigned to the priestly family of Aaron (21:17), so it became a center for training in God's Word and worship. When Solomon became king, the tabernacle was at Gibeon (2 Chronicles 1:3,5). One of David's close friends was a Gibeonite (1 Chronicles 12:1,4). When the Jews returned from exile in Babylon, the list of those who could prove Jewish heritage included Gibeonites (Nehemiah 7:25). Gibeonites helped rebuild the walls of Jerusalem (Nehemiah 3:7). Thus, it seems that the Gibeonites were eventually absorbed into the covenant people because, like Rahab, they transferred their allegiance to the Lord.

7. Israel gave the Gibeonites a menial role in the community, but it kept them close to the Lord and His people. What do you learn about God

from the way things eventually worked out for Gibeon?

_____

_____

_____

_____

_____

For Thought and Discussion: Do non-Christians ever do to Christians what Gibeon did to Israel? Have you ever experienced this? If so, how can we guard against it?

8. What were the potential dangers for Israel of the arrangement Joshua was forced to make with Gibeon?

_____

_____

_____

_____

_____

9. Why do you think the story of Gibeon is included in detail in the book of Joshua? What does this episode add to the book's total message?

_____

_____

_____

_____

_____

10. How is this story relevant to us as Christians?

_____

_____

_____

_____

**Optional
Application:** Are you
currently tempted to
make unwise alli-
ances with nonChris-
tian forces, or are you
missing opportunities
to share the gospel
and God's love
because you are
avoiding unbelievers?
How can you keep
these in the balance
God desires? Plan to
"inquire of the LORD"
(9:14) about this.

11. What one insight from this chapter would you
    like to apply to yourself? How do you need to
    grow in this area?

12. What can you do to let this truth affect your
    life?

13. List any questions you have about 9:1-27.

For the group

Warm-up. Ask everyone to think of an example of
how the victory of God's people is currently threat-

102

ened by direct enemy assault. Then ask everyone to think of an example of how it is threatened by infiltration of nonChristian influences.

Questions. The hard part of this lesson is understanding why it was better in God's eyes for Israel to exterminate Canaanites than to make treaties with them. The key is Deuteronomy 7:1-6 and 9:1-6— God wanted to create a new, holy society unstained by pagan values and practices. This society would eventually become a source of cleansing for its neighbors, rather than a source of defilement for it.

Christians have sometimes taken this to mean that they should exterminate the natives in lands they have conquered. You may want to discuss why this is or isn't a valid application of Joshua. Was the annihilation of the Canaanites a unique command to a unique situation in the history of redemption, or is it a norm to be copied literally?

Christians have also applied this concept of making no treaties, alliances, or compromises with the world to a variety of situations. What New Testament teachings balance and clarify this idea of no compromise and no intermingling? Should we reject all aspects of the cultures we live in, and if so, how is that possible?

When you've considered in general how your situation is and isn't like Israel's, make some personal applications. What alliances should you currently be avoiding, and what contact with unbelievers does God want you to have for the sake of evangelism? Which contacts are defiling you, and which ones are bringing light to others?

Worship. Praise God for His holiness that upholds covenants even when He has not authorized them. Thank Him for being able to use even Israel's mistakes for ultimate good. Thank Him for never failing to give adequate guidance if you diligently inquire of Him. Ask Him to show you if you need to avoid an unwise alliance with the world or make one for another's good.

For Further Study:
For more on the war Christians fight, study 2 Corinthians 10:3-6, Ephesians 6:10-20, Philippians 1:27-30, 2 Timothy 2:1-13, 1 Peter 5:8-11.

Who Is the Enemy?

In Joshua 6, 8, 10, and 11 we read about how Israel ruthlessly slaughtered its enemies. In

(continued on page 104)

(continued from page 103)
chapter 12 we find a list of the kings defeated
and slain in that war. Medieval crusaders,
sixteenth-century colonialists and other Christians have applied these events to their own wars
against flesh-and-blood unbelievers. Other Christians have been horrified by this application and
have insisted that our enemies are only spiritual,
never human people. Others feel that our enemies are sometimes human, in addition to spiritual enemies. How can we decide?

On one level, Israel fought human kings and
noblemen, supported by their priests and common people. Behind them, Israel was combatting
the economic, social, political, military and reli-
gious structures that supported the kings and
that they in turn fought to uphold. These structures are what New Testament writers call "the
world." The root meaning of the Greek word
cosmos is "order," and the New Testament uses
this word to name the corrupt world order in
which human beings live as slaves but which
they defend because they think their lives depend
on it. Behind Israel's flesh-and-blood enemies
was this world order that God wanted to
overturn.

And behind the world structures were the
demonic powers or false gods that have always
been the Lord's real foe (Exodus 12:12, Isaiah
46:1-13). When Paul writes, "For our struggle is
not against flesh and blood, but against the
rulers, against the authorities, against the powers
of this dark world and against the spiritual forces
of evil in the heavenly realms" (Ephesians 6:12),
he is pointing to those impersonal but powerful
world structures and to those personal, demonic
forces that foster and animate the enslaving
world order.

The familiar triad of enemies in the New
Testament is the flesh, the world, and the devil.
In Ephesians 6:12, Paul emphasizes the world
and the devil. He says that "flesh and blood" in
the sense of physical humans is not our enemy.
But "flesh" in the sense of the sinful human
nature that each of us has *is* our enemy. It

(continued on page 105)

104

(continued from page 104)
includes wrong habits, beliefs, attitudes, crav-
ings, and impulses. Since this flesh is what
makes us vulnerable to serving rather than fighting the corrupt world order and the demonic
forces, we must fight it as well.

We are left with a question: When flesh-and-
blood people are fighting to uphold the order of
the world, the flesh, and the devil, should we
fight them? If so, how? How should we decide
how far to go in fighting nonChristians in any
given situation? When, if ever, are physical warfare and killing justifiable? Second Corinthians
10:3-6 and Ephesians 6:10-20 give some guidelines for our warfare; are there others?

God's battle is to free people from the world,
the flesh, and the devil to live abundant, just,
loving, eternal lives for His glory (John 10:10;
Romans 8:3-4,29). To further this aim is to fight
for God's Kingdom. Liberation must be freedom
to be ruled by God (Romans 6:15-23); any other
new society is a deception. As Joshua learned
(Joshua 5:13-15), we cannot enlist God to be on
our side. We must constantly make sure that we
are on His side, fighting His enemies, with His
means, for His ends.

1. Woudstra, pages 84-85.

JOSHUA 10:1-12:24

God Fights for Israel

"When the people of Gibeon heard what Joshua had done to Jericho and Ai, they resorted to a ruse" (9:3-4). For His own reasons, God had allowed them to escape. But for the dissolute kings in their fortresses God had decreed judgment. Their intended all-Canaan alliance (9:1-2) never came off, for by ruling Ai, Bethel, and the Gibeonite league, Joshua controlled the central highlands and had cut the land in two. So, the kings saw no choice but to form two separate coalitions, first in the south and then in the north, to defeat Israel. But "the LORD was fighting for Israel" (10:14), and the outcome was inevitable.

Read 10:1-12:24.

For Thought and Discussion: What does 10:6-9 tell you about covenants?

The battle at Gibeon (10:1-28)

1. The king of Jerusalem was alarmed that Gibeon had gone over to the Israelite side (10:1-2). What did he do about his concern (10:3-5)?

_____

_____

_____

_____

_____

_____

For Thought and Discussion: Compare lesson eight, question 2 to lesson ten, question 3. What similarities and differences do you observe? Is this a pattern that says something about our warfare also?

2. In light of 9:18-20, why do you think Joshua was so quick to come to Gibeon's rescue (10:6-9)?

_____

_____

_____

_____

_____

All-night march (10:9). Joshua led his troops in a swift twenty-mile march from Gilgal to Gibeon, up a road which ascends some 3300 feet.[1] He then threw them (probably exhausted) into battle, and they fought throughout an exceptionally long day (10:12-21,28).

---

3. What part did each of the following play in the victory over the southern coalition?

the Lord (10:8,10-14) _____

_____

_____

_____

_____

Joshua (10:7,9,12,17-28) _____

_____

_____

_____

_____

all Israel (10:7,9-10,18-21,28) _____

_____

_____

_____

_____

_____

_____

Optional Application: a. Does God fight for the Body of Christ now the way He fought for Israel? Have you ever experienced this? If so, describe your experience. If not, can you think of reasons why not?

b. Are you doing your part in God's warfare as thoroughly as Israel did under Joshua? Talk to God about what your part is, and ask for the strength and steadfastness to do your job and rely on His grace for victory.

The sun stood still (10:13). Apparently sometime in the morning of the battle, Joshua prayed to the Lord in the form of giving direct exhortations to the sun and moon (compare Matthew 21:21-22). In much the same way as we talk of the sun rising and setting, rather than the earth rotating, Joshua told the sun and moon to halt in their courses. From where Joshua was standing, the sun was ***over Gibeon*** (10:12) to the southeast, and the moon was ***over the Valley of Aijalon*** to the southwest.

There have been dozens of attempts to reconcile this account with what we know of astronomic physics. Some have shown that the precise words used need not mean "stood still" and "stopped"; they can mean "rest" or "stop [shining]" in the sense of darkening, so that a long, cool, dark day allowed prolonged fighting. This darkness was accompanied by hail and perhaps thunder and lightning (10:11).[2] On the other hand, God created the world and "assigned to each heavenly body its place and function" (see Genesis 1:16).[3] Hence, He is perfectly able to make a day longer without causing the natural disasters or scientific contradictions that men would run into if they tried to do it. All we need know for certain about this event is that it required some extraordinary divine intervention to allow Israel to defeat its enemies.

The Book of Jashar (10:13). "Jashar" could be a person's name, or it could mean "upright,"

109

For Thought and Discussion: a. What does 10:22-28 tell you about Joshua?

b. Is this an example for us in dealing with unbelievers who oppose us? Why or why not? (See Luke 6:27-36, Romans 12:14-21.)

c. Is this an example for dealing with enemies who are not human but spiritual? How, or why not?

d. Is this a record of what did happen that is not a model for what should always happen? Why or why not?

"just." This "work appears to have been a collection of odes in praise of certain heroes" of Israel, "interwoven with historical notices of their achievements."[4] The book itself is lost and is not part of Scripture, but the authors of Joshua and 2 Samuel quote it.

Put your feet on the necks (10:24). "A widespread ancient custom called for victorious kings to put their feet upon the necks of conquered enemies."[5] The aim was to publicly humiliate the foes. The ancients considered the foot to be the lowest part of the body in status as well as physically. The head (and after it, the neck) was the most honorable, exalted part. Hence, this gesture implied that the enemy's most honorable parts were lower than the victor's least ones. (Compare Psalm 110:1, 1 Corinthians 15:24-28.)

Hung them on five trees (10:26). As in 8:29, Joshua had the kings' bodies impaled on trees to show that they were accursed by God (Deuteronomy 21:22-23). As with Jericho, Achan's household, and the king of Ai, the kings' grave becomes another monument testifying to the way the land was conquered.

The southern campaign completed [6]
(10:29-43)

4. Describe the pattern you observe in 10:29-43. What elements are repeated in the accounts of each conquest?

_____

_____

_____

_____

_____

_____

For Further Study:
a. What enemies will Christ put under His feet (1 Corinthians 15:24-28)?
b. What enemies has God already put under Christ's feet (Ephesians 1:19-23)? How have Christ and the Father accomplished this? What are the implications for our lives now?

For Thought and Discussion: What variations do you notice in the pattern of 10:29-43?

_____

_____

_____

_____

The northern campaign (11:1-23)

Hazor (11:1). As in 9:1 and 10:1, trouble started when a king *heard* of what Israel had accomplished. In this case, the king of Hazor heard of what happened in the south. Hazor was a key city in northern Palestine, centered on the trade route from Egypt to Assyria. It was by far the largest and best fortified city in Canaan—the tell (the mound on which the city-fortress was built) covered about thirty acres, and a lower city to the north covered about a hundred seventy-five acres.[7]

Horses and chariots (11:4). Troops in chariots (not mounted cavalry) were "the essential . . . arm of the military forces in the Near East. Each little Canaanite state had its chariots and charioteers."[8] By contrast, Israel was not supposed to rely on horses and chariots (Deuteronomy 17:16, Psalm 20:7), so the Lord told Joshua *to hamstring their horses and burn their chariots* (11:6). Cutting a horse's tendon above the hock or ankle made it unable to walk. Some have found this senseless cruelty, claiming that it subjected the animal to a slow death. However, others say that hamstringing "does not seem to have been unusual, its purpose being to make them unfit as warhorses and employable only for domestic occupations."[9] In either case, God's aim was to keep Israel from trusting in the latest military hardware.

Did not burn (11:13). Like Jericho, Hazor was subjected to the full rigors of *herem* as an example. The lesser northern cities were left standing so that Israelites could live in them (Deuteronomy

111

For Thought and Discussion: Why do you think the author gives us only snap-shot descriptions of most of the southern and all of the northern campaigns (10:29-11:15)? What effect does his method produce?

For Thought and Discussion: a. What important point does the author stress in 11:15?
b. Why is this important?

6:10), and their booty and cattle were left for Israel. Apparently the homes and goods of Canaanites were not necessarily tainted, provided that Israel carefully obeyed God in each instance and avoided idolatry.

5. How is 11:1-15 like the pattern you observed in chapter 10?

_____

_____

_____

_____

_____

_____

6. What points do you think the author is making in his accounts of the southern and northern campaigns? (Think about what you wrote in questions 3 through 5.)

_____

_____

_____

_____

_____

_____

_____

For a long time (11:18). Since Caleb was seventy-eight years old when the conquest began (Deuteronomy 2:14, Joshua 14:7) and eighty-five when he took Hebron (Joshua 14:10), we calculate that the conquest from 6:1 to 11:15 took about seven years.

7. Why did the southern and northern kings decide to fight Israel rather than try to make treaties, as Gibeon did (11:20)?

_____

_____

_____

_____

8. Why did God want this to happen (Genesis 15:16, Deuteronomy 9:4)?

_____

_____

_____

_____

_____

9. In your judgment, does Joshua 11:20 relieve the Canaanites of moral responsibility for their actions? Why or why not?

_____

_____

_____

_____

_____

_____

Optional Application: a. Think of a battle for God's Kingdom in which you are engaged. (Who or what are you fighting against?)

b. What roles do each of the following have in this battle: the Lord; leaders of Christian groups you belong to; fellow members of Christian groups; you?

c. How is this like and unlike the pattern you observed in 10:1-11:15 and in other of Israel's battles?

d. Do you tend to fight alone or in an army of fellow believers? Why? To what extent is your approach biblical and wise?

e. How can you be sure you are fighting the battles the Lord has chosen, in the manner He wants, and relying on His power rather than your own skills?

Study Skill—Hebrew Thought

Europeans and Americans are raised with a system of thought that originated in ancient Greece. This system stresses logic—the kind mathematicians use to deduce axioms in geometry, and the kind Sherlock Holmes made famous for solving crimes. Greek logic insists that opposites contradict each other

(continued on page 114)

For Thought and Discussion: a. What is chapter 12 about?

b. Why do you think the author of Joshua included this list in his book? What is the point of the chapter in the context of the whole book?

(continued from page 113)
and cannot both be true.

By contrast, Hebrews believed that opposites are often both true. In the Bible we find Jesus, the apostles, and the prophets often holding apparently conflicting ideas in tension. For instance, to the Hebrew mind it was deeply true and utterly reasonable to say that God hardened Pharaoh's heart and that Pharaoh hardened his own heart (Exodus 8:32, 9:12). The same was true of the Canaanite kings.

10. What can Joshua 11:20 teach us about the Lord's nature?

_____

_____

_____

_____

_____

_____

Summary and review (11:23-12:24)

11. Joshua 11:23 tells us the goal of all the bloodshed in chapters 6 through 11. What was that goal, and why is it important for us to remember this?

_____

_____

_____

_____

_____

_____

_____

12. What one insight from 10:1-12:24 would you like to focus on this week?

_____

_____

_____

_____

_____

13. How is this truth relevant to your life? How do you need to grow in this area?

_____

_____

_____

_____

_____

14. What can you do to begin letting this insight affect your life this week?

_____

_____

_____

_____

_____

15. List any questions you have about 10:1-12:24.

_____

_____

_____

_____

For Thought and Discussion: a. From 11:23, what would you say that 5:13-12:24 as a whole is about?

b. Use this summary statement to guide you in outlining this section. Give a title to each episode, then group them together or break them down further if you like. (Questions 5 and 6 of lesson one should help you greatly in making an outline.)

115

For the group

Warm-up. Ask each person to describe briefly one battle for God's Kingdom in which he or she is currently engaged. If group members still don't understand what this means for them, ask what they are doing to lay hold of their inheritance or how they are helping to fight God's battles by God's power. It may be that many members will find that they are not doing anything to participate in the spiritual war God has given to the Body of Christ. Or, it may be that some members don't see how what they are already doing furthers God's cause. When you get to application, you can tackle each of these problems and look for ways your group is fighting and can fight God's battles.

Read aloud and summarize. Ask someone to read chapter 10 and someone else to read chapter 11. You can probably omit reading chapter 12. Many Bible dictionaries offer help to pronounce the names of people and places. If you don't have one, encourage readers to do their best and not worry about mispronouncing.

Questions. Don't get bogged down discussing how the Lord made the sun stop. Instead, focus on what chapters 10 through 12 are meant to teach us about how Israel took the land. Don't spiritualize the text by jumping straight to application, and don't gloss over the shocking parts (humiliating the kings, impaling their bodies, hamstringing the horses, executing women and children). What do these events reveal about the Lord? How can you hold them in harmony and tension with His love and mercy? Why did He harden the hearts of Canaan's kings? Why did He want Israel to wipe out the Canaanites and take their land?

When you've wrestled with the literal historical events, then turn to application. The box on pages 103-105 may help you identify the battles God has given you. To what extent are God's commands and actions in chapters 10 and 11 unique to that time, and to what extent are they like what He does and commands today? How can you decide? What do these chapters motivate you to do individually and as a group? In your worship time, pray about this.

116

Worship. Praise God for fighting miraculously for Israel, for hardening the hearts of the wicked kings of Canaan, and for crushing their world and replacing it with His godly society. Praise His power and justice. Thank Him for having mercy on you, for welcoming you into His Kingdom like Rahab and Gibeon, rather than exterminating you like the other Canaanites. Ask Him to guide you in continuing to help spread His rule on the earth.

1. Hamlin, page 86; Woudstra, page 171.
2. Woudstra, pages 175-176, note 33; *The NIV Study Bible*, page 305; Hamlin, pages 87-88.
3. Woudstra, page 176.
4. Woudstra, page 176.
5. Woudstra, page 178.
6. For detailed information on each place, see Woudstra, pages 179-183.
7. Woudstra, page 187; *The NIV Study Bible*, page 306.
8. Woudstra, page 190.
9. H. Freedman, *Joshua*, in *Joshua and Ruth*, edited by A. Cohen (London, 1950), page 64; see Woudstra, page 192, footnote 24.

Allotments for the Twelve Tribes

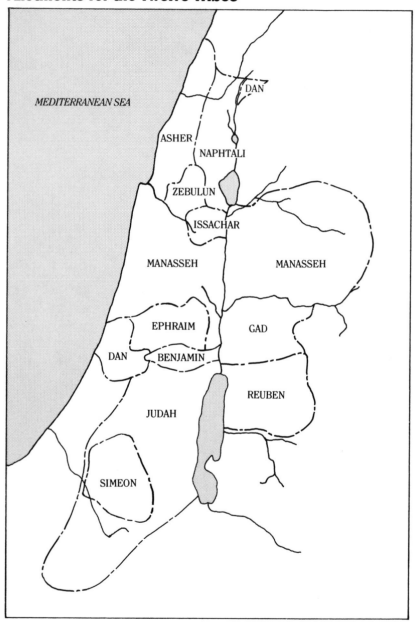

JOSHUA 13:1-17:18

Inheritances

After the key campaigns, "the land had rest from war" (11:23) because the unified resistance of the cities was broken. God had made good on His promise to give Israel the land. But there was more work to be done. As you read 13:1-17:18, don't get mired in the names of people and places. Look for the overall sweep of the story and the little comments and incidents the author records in the midst of the data.

Much of chapters 13 through 21 is like a formal royal land grant, the administrative record of the King's gift to loyal subjects who helped Him conquer the territory. For the general outline of areas assigned to each tribe, see the map on page 118. (For more specific information about the places named, see Woudstra, pages 208-315.) We will be taking a broad overview of these chapters to see what main points the author is trying to make. At the same time, we will focus in on some of the little episodes the author recounts to see why he thought them important.

Old (13:1). Probably around ninety years old, since Caleb was eighty-five (14:10) and Joshua died at one hundred and ten.

The land that remains (13:2-5). God outlines the territory to the south, along the west coast, and to the north, most of it in Philistine or Phoeni-

119

Optional Application: Read Psalm 16:5-6. What is your lot, portion, and inheritance? How does knowing this affect your priorities and actions?

cian hands. The book of Joshua holds a seeming contradiction in tension: on one hand, "Joshua took the entire land" (11:23); on the other hand, "there are still very large areas of land to be taken over" (13:1). This "already but not yet" is also true of the Kingdom which God has promised us.

Allocate (13:6). ("Divide . . . by lot" in KJV.) Literally, "cause to fall." That is, the land was assigned by means of casting lots. Since God ruled the lot (Proverbs 16:33), this method allowed the King to divide His domain as He chose.[1]

Divide (13:7). This Hebrew word is from the same root as "portion" in Joshua 17:14. With this word and the double use of "inheritance" in 13:6-7, God stresses His gracious gift to His beloved people. (See Psalm 16:5-6 and Isaiah 61:7 for the spiritual connotations of these terms.)[2]

1. Why do you think the author includes so much detail about which land was allotted to each tribe? How does this contribute to the themes of the book (1:6, 11:23, 21:43-45)?

_____

_____

_____

_____

_____

_____

Clan by clan (13:15,23,24,28,29,31; 15:1,20; 16:5; 18:11; 19:1,16,17,23,24,31,32,39,40,48). In the Canaanite system of land management, the nobility controlled the land and common people were constantly subject to "debt slavery, sharecropping, and economic hardship."[3] By contrast, the Israelite system gave each group of extended families, called a "clan" or "father's house," control of a piece of land. The clan assigned parcels to each member family. Every fifty years, the land was redistributed within the clan according to the growth or shrinkage of families. It was illegal to sell land outside the clan; it could only be leased for up to forty-nine years (Leviticus 25:1-55).

The clan was also responsible for caring for poor member families by giving them interest-free loans and limiting debt slavery to seven years (Deuteronomy 15:1-11). Finally, the clan had military duties: each clan had to send one unit of soldiers to the army. Thus, the clan played a crucial role in the Israel God wanted to build, so the author of Joshua stressed the allotment by clans.

For Further Study:
Using a concordance, investigate the use and meaning of the number twelve in the Old and New Testaments. What might be the significance of twelve?

2. The territory for the two-and-a-half tribes east of the Jordan was allocated years earlier (Numbers 32:1-42). Why do you suppose the author includes a record of that allotment in 13:8-33, before recording the inheritances of the other tribes?

_____

_____

_____

_____

_____

_____

Nine-and-a-half (14:2). The twelve-tribe structure of Israel was important to God for some reason. Therefore, the author takes pains to explain how the twelve was maintained. Levi was set apart to be the tribe of priests and teachers of the Law, so the Levites would live off the tithes and offerings rather than by farming. That left eleven tribes. To fill up the number, Joseph was divided into two tribes, the descendants of

121

Joseph's two sons, Ephraim and Manasseh. Out of love for Joseph, his father Jacob had adopted Ephraim and Manasseh as his own sons and promised them equal inheritance with his other sons (Genesis 48:5).

Judah (14:6). Reuben had forfeited the rights of the firstborn by sinning against his father (Genesis 35:22, 49:3-4). So, Jacob gave the double inheritance to Joseph, the firstborn of his second wife, by adopting Ephraim and Manasseh. However, there remained the firstborn's right to lead the family. Simeon and Levi were born second and third after Reuben, but they shamed the family by deceiving and slaughtering the men of Shechem (Genesis 34). For this sin, Jacob decreed that they would be scattered among the tribes. Simeon received only cities within the territory assigned to Judah (Joshua 19:1-9) and eventually was absorbed and disappeared. The Levites received towns throughout Israel, but because Levi was the only tribe to reject idolatry at Sinai, God turned the curse of scattering into a blessing (Exodus 32:25-29) by making Levi His special inheritance. But the setting aside of Reuben, Simeon, and Levi left Jacob's fourth son, Judah, to inherit the rule of the family (Genesis 49:8-12). Therefore, Judah received the first allotment west of the Jordan, and eventually the kings of David's line came from Judah.

3. Flanking the account of Judah's allotment is the record of Joshua giving (14:6-15) and Caleb taking (15:13-19) Caleb's inheritance.

   a. Describe Caleb's attitude toward the Lord's commands and promises, and how he showed that attitude (14:6-12, 15:14-16).

   _____

   _____

   _____

   _____

   _____

_____

_____

b. What were the results of Caleb's attitudes and
the Lord's actions?

_____

_____

_____

_____

c. Why do you think these events merit special
mention in light of the whole message of the
book? (Consider 21:45.)

_____

_____

_____

_____

_____

Springs of water (15:19). The Negev is semi-arid,
almost desert in dry years. It is workable land
provided that one has access to water other
than the fickle rains. Caleb gave his daughter a
field as a dowry, but she realized that it was
worthless without a water supply.

Water was a powerful symbol for agricul-
tural people in a hot, dry climate. It was an
ordinary, physical substance, but never taken
for granted. The author of Joshua must have
been thinking of what this life-giving liquid
meant to Israel in relation to the Lord's promises (Deuteronomy 8:7; 28:15,22-24; Psalm
63:1; Isaiah 1:29-30; 12:1-3; 41:17-20).

Joseph (16:1). By Jacob's will, Joseph received first
priority after Judah. Ordinarily, Joseph's firstborn would have received his inheritance first.

For Thought and Discussion: Why do you think the story of Acsah's water is recorded for us (15:15-19)? What does it reveal about the Lord's concerns? How is it a parable for us?

Optional Application: a. The author seems to tell Caleb's story in part as a contrast to the rest of Judah, Ephraim, and Manasseh. How was Caleb different?

b. How can you be more like Caleb and less like the other tribes?

However, Jacob chose to give priority to Ephraim over Manasseh when he adopted them (Genesis 48:14,19), so 16:5-10 precedes 17:1-13. Manasseh had only one son, so effectively the allotment for Manasseh was for Makir (17:1).

These details may seem dull to us, but they emphasize the legality of the land grants and the fulfillment of prophecies Jacob received centuries earlier.

---

4. Caleb was able to drive out the fierce Anakites (15:14), but the rest of Judah was unable to drive out the Jebusites (15:63). So, Judah was content to live among the pagans. Even when Ephraim and Manasseh were strong enough to drive out Canaanites in their territories, they settled for reducing the pagans to forced labor, which raised Israel's standard of living (16:10, 17:12-13).

What do these facts tell you about the faith and priorities of these tribes, as compared to Caleb's?

_____

_____

_____

_____

_____

_____

_____

Daughters (17:3). Like Caleb's daughter (15:19), Zelophehad's daughters had their eyes on practical needs. They could have provided for themselves by marrying, but to let their father's name die out from his clan was a tragedy in that family-oriented culture. Also, their children would have no inheritance. So, they went to Moses ten or more years ago to win the right to inherit alongside the men of their clan

124

(Numbers 27:1-11). This required an amendment to the law that said only men could inherit—lobbying for amended legislation was a bold thing for Near Eastern women to attempt. But the Lord honored their commitment to past and future generations.

Forest (17:15). Centuries of abuse have stripped Palestine barren, and modern Israel struggles to reforest the hills. But in Joshua's time much of the hill country was dense thickets. Before irrigation channels could be dug and the hills terraced for farming, those woods had to be cleared. Wild animals, briars, and sheer density made this a monumental task. The Canaanites had barely begun it; the hill country was one of the most sparsely settled areas.

On the other hand, forests were considered a "splendor" in a land (Isaiah 10:18, compare 2 Kings 19:23), a valuable resource. Losing the forests was one of the curses God would send when Israel broke covenant (Isaiah 2:13, Jeremiah 21:14), and God would show His forgiveness by restoring the trees (Isaiah 41:19). At the same time, having cultivated land revert to wild forest thickets would be a sign of God's judgment (Hosea 2:12), and the taming of this wild land into park land would herald God's new creation (Isaiah 55:12-13). In short, the forests had rich meanings for Israel that grew out of the very basic, literal task Joshua gave to Joseph: turn the wild forest into a place where people can live in abundance and beauty, like the treed park God gave Adam to work and care for (Genesis 2:8-9,15; Joshua 17:18).

For Further Study: In your judgment, how does God want us to treat our human neighbors who are not Christians? Should we exterminate or subjugate them? Live among them and copy their practices? Tolerate their presence with as few social contacts as possible? Exploit their labor without taking any personal interest in them or their spiritual lives? Make friends with them but ignore their lifestyles? Use the New Testament to form your view, then look for ways it applies to how you relate to your neighbors. (For instance, examine Matthew 5:13-16,43-48; 28:18-20; Romans 12:2; 15:1-3; 1 Corinthians 10:23-11:1; Ephesians 4:17-5:20; Titus 3:1-2; 1 Peter 3:15-16.)

5. The tribes of Joseph were disappointed at their apparently meager inheritance because they valued it on the basis of what men had already done with it (cities, cleared farmland, etc.). What did Joshua suggest (17:14-18)?

_____

_____

_____

For Thought and Discussion: How are Zelophehad's daughters models for women and men today? How can we act to ensure the inheritances of future generations?

For Further Study: Using a concordance, research the symbolic meanings of forests in the Old Testament. (Look up *tree, forest, thicket, pine,* etc.)

6. In your judgment, what attitudes toward God, self, and God's gifts did the house of Joseph show (17:16)?

7. We have focused on some of the little episodes, like parables, hidden in the legal documents of 13:1-17:18. What one insight from what you have studied would you like to concentrate on this week?

8. How is this relevant to you? How do you need to grow in this area?

9. What practical steps can you take to make this a part of your life?

_____

_____

_____

_____

_____

_____

10. If you have any questions about 13:1-17:18, write them down.

_____

_____

_____

_____

Optional Application: a. Are you in any ways like the tribes of Joseph in 17:14-18? If so, how?
b. How is Joshua's counsel relevant to you? What land should you have the courage and faith to turn into God's garden, despite seemingly fierce enemies?

For the group

Warm-up. Ask everyone to think of one thing God has promised him or her that he or she has not yet received.

Read aloud. Assign the following excerpts to different readers: 13:1,6-8; 14:1-15; 15:13-19,63; 17:3-6,12-18.

Summarize.

Questions. Try to cover all the numbered questions 1-6. Then give each person a chance to tell which incident or detail struck him or her as personally significant. Take some time to discuss those incidents: what is important to you about them, why you think the author made special mention of them, and what they motivate you to do.

Summarize. What overall thread or themes do you see running through the details you noticed in 13:1-17:18? What seems to be the main message to you?

Worship. Praise God for being utterly faithful to His promises to Israel. Thank Him for showing you what He can do with a person like Caleb, and what happens when people are like the tribes of Judah and Joseph. Thank Him for His concern for water, future generations, women—the needs of all His people. Thank Him for enabling each of you to take possession of your inheritances.

1. Woudstra, page 213, note 15.
2. Woudstra, page 213.
3. Hamlin, pages 111-112.

JOSHUA 18:1-21:45

God's Provisions

When God said it was time to allocate the land, you
might think the tribes would line up to receive their
portions. Not so. Caleb the ever-faithful was on
Joshua's doorstep to claim the promises God gave
him, then he led his family out to wrest his land
from the Canaanites. The rest of Judah showed up
promptly for their allotments, although they were
less successful than Caleb in taking possession.
Likewise were the tribes of Joseph, who even
grumbled about the measly portion they thought
they were getting. The other seven tribes didn't
even ask for their shares. At an all-Israel meeting at
Shiloh, Joshua was finally fed up and took action.
To see what he did, read 18:1-21:45.

Allotments for the seven tribes and Joshua (18:1-19:51)

Shiloh (18:1). The town was twelve miles south of
Shechem in Ephraim's territory, centrally
located for all the tribes to come.[1]

Tent of Meeting (18:1). The tabernacle or tent that
housed the ark of the covenant. The daily sacrifices were held there, and it was the focal point
of national gatherings.

1. What attitude did Joshua imply that the seven

Optional Application: Ask the Lord if you are like the seven tribes in any way.

tribes were showing (18:3)?

_____

_____

_____

_____

_____

_____

2. Examine how the allotment to the seven was carried out (18:4-10). What do you think were the aims of this method?

_____

_____

_____

_____

_____

_____

_____

Simeon (19:1) Recall from page 122 that Simeon received only cities within Judah because the tribe was destined to be scattered for its forefather's sin.

Joshua (19:49). As Caleb's portion began the record of the allotments (14:6), so Joshua's ends it. These accounts of rewarded faithfulness flank the less sterling records in between. **Timnath Serah** (19:50) was in the southwest corner of Joshua's tribe of Ephraim, facing the sea. It was no grand domain fit for the warlord of a conquering army, but a humble patrimony for a loyal servant of God. An eastern general usually took his share of the spoils first, but Joshua took his last.[2]

3. How is Joshua a model for Christian leaders in
   19:49-50?

   _____

   _____

   _____

   _____

   _____

   _____

Cities of refuge (20:1-9)

Cities of refuge (20:2). Killing an innocent person
was considered a terrible offense that polluted
the land because humans were made in God's
image (Genesis 9:5-6, Numbers 35:33). Animal
sacrifice could not atone for willful murder; it
demanded the death penalty. The person
responsible for carrying out that sentence was
the murdered person's nearest male relative,
called *the avenger of blood* (Joshua 20:3;
Numbers 35:16-21), not the state.

However, if someone killed another acci-
dentally, the avenger of blood was still bound to
slay the killer to cleanse the land from the pol-
lution of innocent blood. Yet if he did this, he
would himself become guilty of shedding innocent blood. A feud might thus destroy whole
families and defile the land horribly. To avoid
this, God had cities in each region set aside to
which an accidental killer could flee. There he
could find welcome and safety until his trial,
there he was assured a fair trial away from the
family home of the dead person, and there he
could make a living until he was free to go
home. There were careful procedures for the
trial to see that justice was done (Numbers
35:6,15-30; Deuteronomy 19:1-13). A mistake
was not to be punished like a crime, but it did
have consequences.

The six cities chosen were all assigned to
the Levites (20:7-8; 21:3,11,21,27,32,36,38), so

it would be their task to welcome the refugee, protect him, and give him a fair trial (20:4-6). There was bound to be work available that a non-Levite could do.

The cities were "in central places on both sides of the Jordan, so they were easy to reach from any place in the country. God expressly commanded that roads were to be made to these cities (Deuteronomy 19:3). . . . [The highways] were carefully repaired every spring, after the rains and bad weather of winter. Further, bridges were built where needed so that a man did not have to run down into a ravine but could go straight across, taking the shortest possible route to the city. At every crossroad were special signs which said, 'Refuge! Refuge!' and pointed in the direction of the city. They had to be large enough so that a man running [from an avenging pursuer] could easily read them."[3]

Also, the cities were available to everyone, to travelers and resident foreigners as well as Israelites (Numbers 35:15). Their doors were never locked.[4]

It is not clear why **the death of the high priest** (20:6) marked the end of the killer's exile. The high priest was anointed with the holy oil and performed the annual atonement sacrifices, so his death may have had some power to atone for accidental bloodguilt. Or, his death may have marked the end of an epoch, a sort of statute of limitations. Other possibilities abound.[5]

---

4. What important truths about God—His character, values, justice—do you learn from the institution of the cities of refuge?

_____

_____

_____

_____

_____

_____

5. Hebrews 6:18 says that we "have fled to take hold of the hope" of salvation in Christ. How is Christ like and unlike a city of refuge for us?

like _____

_____

_____

_____

_____

unlike _____

_____

_____

_____

_____

Cities for the Levites (21:1-45)

Levites (21:1). The author has stressed that Levi received no land as an inheritance, but only cities with surrounding pastures (13:14, 14:4, 18:7). Instead, the Lord Himself and the fruits of their service to Him were their inheritance. They lived primarily off the tithes and offerings each Israelite gave (Numbers 18:21-24, Deuteronomy 18:1-2). Some of the Levites were priests who spent their time performing the daily rites. Others were responsible for caring for the tabernacle, its furnishings, and all the administrative work that the massive system required. But most Levites lived in the forty-eight cities scattered throughout Israel. Their job was to study and teach God's Word, as well as to be health inspectors and fill other roles that required literacy (Leviticus 13:1-14:57, Deuteronomy 31:9-13).

The Levites did not own their cities, but merely used them as God's gift, to remind all Israel that their real inheritance was the Lord and the land was His gift (Psalm 16:5).

6. Why do you think the Lord wanted cities in each tribe inhabited by students of His Word and men devoted to His worship? Why didn't He put all the Levites in one place?

_____

_____

_____

_____

_____

_____

7. Why do you think He put the Levites in charge of the cities of refuge? Why was this job appropriate for them?

_____

_____

_____

_____

_____

_____

8. Why is 21:43-45 an appropriate conclusion to 13:1-21:45, which deals with the allotments?

_____

_____

_____

_____

_____

9. Why doesn't 13:1 contradict 21:43-45 and 11:23? How were both perspectives true and important to remember?

_____

_____

_____

_____

_____

_____

Optional Application: How are both perspectives in question 9 true and important to remember in your life?

10. What truth from 18:1-21:45 strikes you as something you want to take to heart?

_____

_____

_____

_____

_____

11. How is this insight relevant to your life? How do you want it to affect you?

_____

_____

_____

_____

_____

12. What can you do this week to begin letting this truth accomplish its work in you?

_____

_____

_____

_____

13. List any questions you have about 18:1-21:45.

For the group

Warm-up. Ask, "How have you experienced God's compassion or provision for your needs during the past week?" Like 13:1-17:18, 18:1-21:45 is full of ways in which God provided compassionately for Israel's needs.

Read aloud. Read 18:1-10; 19:49-51; 20:1-9; 21:1-8,41-45.

Summarize.

Questions. There are several "why" questions in this lesson because the author of Joshua leaves the meaning of the events for the reader to interpret. As in the last lesson, you need to know a lot more about what was going on than the passages in Joshua tell you if you are going to avoid wild specu-lation. The background and cross-references in this study guide should help you answer the questions. The goal of them all is to see what you learn about God from the provisions He makes for the seven tribes, the Levites, and all Israel. Then, what light does this shed on the provisions He constantly makes for you? For application, look for specific ways to respond to what God has done.

Worship. Thank God for the way He provides His people with land to live on, teachers to model and explain His Word, and a refuge from death for their sins and mistakes. Thank Him especially for Christ, your Refuge.

1. Woudstra, page 271.

2. *The NIV Study Bible*, page 318; Jensen, pages 111, 114.
3. Schaeffer, page 196.
4. Schaeffer, page 197.
5. Woudstra, pages 300-301.

JOSHUA 22:1-34

East and West

The land has been taken and divided among the tribes; the promised rest is fulfilled for now. The eastern tribes have shared in the work of conquest and have received their share of the inheritance: land, booty, cities of refuge, Levites in their midst to teach God's Word. They are full members of the covenant nation, despite the physical barrier between their land and Canaan—the Jordan River. Now it is time to settle down to work at peace with the same zeal with which they worked at war. How do you work at peace? Read 22:1-34.

Peace fulfilled (22:1-9)

1. For what does Joshua commend the eastern tribes (22:1-3)?

_____

_____

_____

_____

_____

_____

2. He exhorts them to remain faithful to the covenant they made with God alongside their

For Thought and Discussion: Why do you think the author makes such a point of telling about the eastern tribes' role in the story (1:12-18, 13:8-33, 22:1-34)? How is this connected to his stress on "all Israel"?

139

kinsmen, to continue to keep the Torah (Law, Teaching) of Moses. How does Joshua summarize the Torah in 22:5?

_____

_____

_____

_____

Hold fast (22:5, 23:8). "Cleave" in KJV. This Hebrew word "describes the deep personal attachment that creates a new unity,"[1] as when a man leaves his parents and cleaves to his wife to become "one flesh" (Genesis 2:24). It is the joyful attachment to the beloved that admits no rival lovers. It is a person's response to God's wooing love. The Old Testament often depicts Israel's covenant as a marriage bond.

Heart . . . soul (22:5). Deuteronomy 6:5 instructs Israel to love the Lord "with all your heart and with all your soul and with all your strength." Here Joshua says essentially the same about serving Him. In Hebrew thought, the word *heart* "is used to refer to the power of planning, understanding, memory, judgment, and will." The word *soul* "emphasizes the longing, desiring, striving, thirsting, vulnerable, incomplete aspects of personality."[2] In other words, the Israelites must love and serve God with all their rational and emotional being. Love and service are acts of the mind, the will, and the emotions.

3. What does Jesus think about Joshua's summary of the Torah (Deuteronomy 6:5, Joshua 22:5, Matthew 22:34-40)?

_____

_____

_____

140

4. What do loving, walking, obeying, holding fast, and serving mean for you this week? In what specific ways do you need to do these things currently? Pray about this.

_____

_____

_____

_____

_____

_____

Divide with your brothers (22:8). Some warriors apparently stayed back to guard the women, children, and property. Those support troops were just as important a part of the fighting force as the front line troops.

Peace threatened (22:10-34)

Geliloth (22:10). The site is uncertain, but east of Shiloh along the Jordan is likely.[3] NASB and RSV read "the region of the Jordan" instead of "Geliloth near the Jordan."

Sin of Peor (22:17). In Moab, some Israelites had participated in debauched worship of the Baal of Peor and were executed (Numbers 25:1-9).

5. What did the western tribes think the altar at Geliloth signified (22:15-19)?

_____

_____

_____

_____

For Thought and Discussion: What were the western tribes offering to give up in 22:19? What does this tell you about their priorities?

For Thought and Discussion: What did all Israel know about fearing the Holy Lord (22:16-29)?

6. How did they handle the crisis?

22:11-12 _____

_____

_____

22:13-20 _____

_____

_____

_____

7. What do you think of this response? Was it appropriate, godly, and loving, or not? Why? (*Optional:* Evaluate Israel's conduct by 1 Corinthians 5:1-2, Colossians 3:12-14, Hebrews 12:14-17.)

_____

_____

_____

_____

_____

_____

The LORD's land (22:19). "The promised land proper had never included Transjordan territory. Canaan was the land the Lord especially claimed as his own and promised to the descendants of Abraham, Isaac and Jacob."[4]

The Mighty One, God, the LORD! (22:22). In Hebrew, *El Elohim Yahweh*. This triple name, twice invoked, forms a solemn, weighty oath in the name of the All-knowing God.

Witness (22:27). This is the sixth monument recorded in Joshua that was built to remind Israel of something. The long name in 22:34 was typical for Near Eastern monuments.

142

8. How did the eastern tribes react to the grave charges against them?

22:21-23 _____

_____

_____

_____

22:24-29 _____

_____

_____

_____

9. What do you think of the reasoning that led the easterners to build the altar?

_____

_____

_____

_____

_____

_____

10. Both the eastern and western tribes were passionately concerned with unity (22:18-20,24-28). Why was unity so important to both sides?

_____

_____

_____

_____

_____

_____

For Thought and Discussion: a. Is unity as important in the Body of Christ as it was in Israel? Why or why not (John 17:20-23, Ephesians 4:1-16)?
  b. What are some implications for your life?

For Thought and Discussion: Did the tribes speak "the truth in love" (Ephesians 4:15) to each other? Support your opinion.

11. Phinehas saw the easterners' answer as evidence "that the LORD is with us" (22:31). Why was it evidence of this?

_____

_____

_____

_____

12. What would you say is the point of chapter 22? What does it contribute to the themes and overall message of Joshua?

_____

_____

_____

_____

_____

13. What can we learn from this story that is relevant to us as Christians?

_____

_____

_____

_____

_____

_____

14. What one truth from chapter 22 would you like to take to heart?

_____

_____

_____

_____

_____

15. How is it relevant to your life? How do you need to grow in this area?

_____

_____

_____

_____

_____

16. What can you do to begin applying this truth?

_____

_____

_____

_____

_____

17. List any questions you have about 22:1-34.

_____

_____

_____

_____

For the group

Warm-up. Ask, "Think of a dispute or threat to unity—past or present—that you have observed in your church or fellowship." Give everyone a minute or two to think, but don't take a lot of time to share answers.

Read aloud and summarize.

Peace fulfilled. The return home of the eastern tribes closes the frame begun in 1:12-18. Be sure to discuss what you think the author's point is in telling about the easterners' faithfulness to their promise and their release from that promise now that rest has been achieved. Questions 2-4 focus in on 22:5 because it is particularly relevant to Christians. We can view 22:1-3 as an application of the command to love and serve God (and to love one's neighbor) to the situation at hand. Because 22:5 is the essence of the Torah, it deserves some attention.

Peace threatened. Here we find a threat to the unity and rest Joshua extolled in 22:1-9. The questions ask you to observe what happened and to evaluate each side's handling of the situation. Point out the implications of unity: because Israel is one people, the westerners will suffer if the easterners sin (22:18-20; compare chapter 7); therefore, it is in everyone's interest to see that righteousness, peace, and unity are upheld. Unity isn't just a goal for Israel; it is a present fact to be dealt with. Both east and west do what they do because they are afraid of the other breaking the nation's unity. When your group has a grip on the issues at stake, see if you can apply what you've learned to similar situations in the Body of Christ today.

Worship. Thank God for establishing and maintaining unity among the different branches of His people. Ask Him to help the Body of Christ come to unity as Israel did in a time of crisis. Ask Him to help the whole Church make utter loyalty to Him as much a priority as it was in Joshua's time. Praise "The Mighty One, God, the LORD," and ask Him to help you hold fast to Him and serve Him with all your heart and soul.

1. Hamlin, page 187.
2. Hamlin, page 188; see also H. W. Wolff, *Anthropology of the Old Testament* (London: SCM, 1974), pages 10-25,46-55.
3. *The NIV Study Bible*, page 320.
4. *The NIV Study Bible*, page 321.

JOSHUA 23:1-16

To the Future

Joshua's job is almost done. As promised (1:6), he has led Israel to inherit the land God swore to their forefathers to give them. The Canaanites are still present, but the Israelites have such a foothold that there is no way they can be expelled. The land has been apportioned to the tribes, and the people have begun to settle down. As Moses did before him, it is time for Joshua to pass the mantle.

Read 23:1-16, looking for the overall point Joshua is making.

Nations (23:3,4,7,9,12,13). Joshua uses this word seven times, a number of fullness. The nations are a major part of what Joshua has to say to the leaders of Israel.

1. Joshua considers it important to remind Israel of what the Lord has done. What has He done (23:3,9-10,14)?

_____

_____

_____

_____

_____

147

_____

_____

2. What has He promised to do (23:4-5)?

_____

_____

_____

_____

3. What must Israel do (and not do) in response (23:6-8,11,12,16)?

do _____

_____

_____

_____

_____

not do _____

_____

_____

_____

4. Joshua repeats three times in almost the same words what will happen if Israel violates this agreement. What will happen (23:13,15-16)?

_____

_____

_____

_____

5. How would you summarize Joshua's main point in 23:1-16?

_____

_____

_____

_____

_____

_____

6. Why do you think he addresses this speech primarily to Israel's leaders (23:2)?

_____

_____

_____

_____

_____

7. In what ways is God's Word to us like His Word to Israel in 23:1-16, and in what ways is it different? Consider one or two of the following aspects. (Be able to give reasons for your view.)

   a. Does the Lord fight for us? If so, describe one way in which you have observed Him doing this. If not, why not?

   _____

   _____

   _____

   _____

   _____

   _____

   b. Has God overcome "nations" to give you living space? If so, explain how He has done this. (For instance, are the nations literal people?) If not, has He done anything at all similar, or did God do this uniquely for Israel?

_____

_____

_____

_____

_____

_____

c. Has God kept His promise so far to give you your inheritance (23:14)? If so, how? If not, why do you think He hasn't?

_____

_____

_____

_____

_____

_____

d. Does God want you "to obey all that is written in the Book of the Law of Moses" (23:6)? If you think so, why? If not, why not, and does He want you to do something similar? (Some relevant cross-references might be Matthew 5:17-20, 22:34-40; John 15:9-14; Romans 13:8-10; Galatians 2:15-16, 3:19-25, 5:13-26; Ephesians 2:11-18.)

_____

_____

_____

_____

_____

_____

_____

_____

e. Are we forbidden to ally with or associate
with unbelievers (Joshua 23:7,12)? If so, in
what senses? If not how is our situation different from Israel's? (You might see Matthew
9:11-13, 28:19; 1 Corinthians 5:9-11; 2 Corinthians 6:14-18.)

_____

_____

_____

_____

_____

_____

f. Joshua gave Israel reasons for loving God
(23:9-11). Why should you love God?

_____

_____

_____

_____

_____

g. In what specific ways can you love God?

_____

_____

_____

_____

_____

For Thought and Discussion: Will you lose your inheritance on earth if you ally with the "nations" or serve their gods (23:12-13,16)? Will you lose your eternal inheritance if you do this? Support your view with the New Testament.

h. What are some of the false gods of our culture? How can you avoid invoking and bowing down to them?

_____

_____

_____

_____

_____

_____

_____

_____

Invoke . . . swear . . . serve . . . bow down (23:7). These words imply a progression: invoking with the *lips*, swearing with upraised *hand*, bending the *knee* in service, and finally prostrating the *whole body* before the false gods. Israel wasn't even supposed to talk about the false gods (Exodus 23:13), but instead to mention and remember the Lord, because talking about something is the first step toward paying serious attention to it. Swearing by something is the next step; it ascribes some power or integrity to the god. Israel was supposed to swear by the Lord and be bound by His integrity (Deuteronomy 6:13). To serve something is to acknowledge its supremacy and to offer it the loyalty owed to God. To prostrate oneself in utter adoration is a total self-offering—the ultimate response to the One God, and the ultimate blasphemy if done to anything else.[1]

---

8. What one insight from 23:1-16 seems most important for you to concentrate on right now?

_____

_____

_____

_____

_____

9. How do you want this to affect you?

_____

_____

_____

_____

10. What action can you take to begin applying this truth?

_____

_____

_____

_____

11. List any questions you have about chapter 23.

_____

_____

_____

_____

For the group

Warm-up. Ask everyone to think of ways in which God has kept His promises to him or her.

Read aloud and summarize.

Questions. Questions 1-6 lead you through observations to see what Joshua had to say to Israel as his farewell. Then question 7 is an exercise in thinking how a passage does and doesn't apply to us today. It might be a bit tedious and time-consuming to cover all eight parts of question 7; use your own judgment about how many to discuss. Be sure to allow time for everyone to share one way in which he or she wants to act on a personal application from this chapter.

Worship. Thank God for fighting for Israel. Praise Him for being utterly faithful to His promises. Ask Him to help you take to heart His insistence on absolute loyalty, love, and obedience.

1. Hamlin, pages 182-185.

JOSHUA 24:1-33

Covenant Renewal

Moses' last official act before his death was to call a new generation of Israelites to renew the covenant their parents made at Sinai. "Choose life," he said, by loving and obeying your Lord (Deuteronomy 30:15,19). In the thirty or so years since then, many of that generation who heard Moses and crossed the Jordan with Joshua have died, and their children have grown up. Now it is Joshua's turn to lay a choice before a new generation and call them to renew their covenant before he departs.

As you read 24:1-33, try to put yourself into Joshua's audience.

Shechem (24:1). The same site as in 8:30-35 was chosen, perhaps because of its excellent acoustics.

This is what the LORD . . . says (24:2). This phrase signals the beginning of a prophecy, and Joshua proceeds to speak for the Lord. But this is prophecy about the past rather than the future; it is the Lord's perspective on history. An ancient covenant between a lord and a vassal often began with a prologue recounting the history of the relationship, particularly the good things the lord had done that should inspire the vassal to loyalty. Archaeologists have found many such written treaties, and Joshua seems to be doing something similar in this speech.

155

For Thought and Discussion: Where would Israel be if the Lord hadn't intervened in Abraham's life, in Egypt, in the desert, and in Canaan (24:2-13)? Why is this important for Israel to remember? Why is it important for you to know?

For Thought and Discussion: What has God been doing in your ancestors' lives for the past seven hundred years? Where would you be if He hadn't done these things?

Balak . . . Balaam (24:9). Numbers 22-24 tells how Balak of Moab sent for Balaam the diviner to curse Israel, but the Lord turned the curse into a blessing. The pagans were trying to work magic, which attempts to manipulate the gods, but the Lord showed that He was above magical manipulation. To teach Israel the difference between magic and true prophetic prayer, the Lord chose to work through a pagan diviner to bless Israel. The word of a true prophet of the Lord does not try to manipulate Him but invites Him to do what He has told the prophet He wants to do (Numbers 23:8,11-12).

Hornet (24:12). The meaning of this Hebrew word is unclear. Some people think it refers to the irrational panic which spread through the Canaanites when they heard about Israel (2:11, 5:1, 9:24).[1]

1. Who is the main character and the subject of almost all the sentences in 24:2-13? Why is this significant?

2. What point does the historical summary in 24:2-13 make?

3. How should Israel respond (24:14)?

_____

_____

_____

_____

4. Why is this the appropriate response?

_____

_____

_____

_____

5. Why is choice (24:15) so important for Israel and for us?

_____

_____

_____

_____

6. Why did Israel choose to serve the Lord (24:16-18)?

_____

_____

_____

_____

7. Consider what Joshua says in 24:19-20. In what sense was Israel able to serve the Lord, and in what sense was Israel not able?

able (Deuteronomy 30:11-16, Joshua 24:14)

_____

_____

Optional Application: Put yourself in Israel's place, and listen to what God has done for you. Thank Him for each thing. Take time to pray about the choice He is laying before you in light of what He has done.

For Thought and Discussion: What gods did your parents serve? What gods are you tempted to serve?

For Thought and Discussion: Is it possible to choose to serve neither the Lord nor other gods? Why or why not? (See Romans 6:15-23.)

157

_____

_____

_____

not able (Joshua 24:19-20) _____

_____

_____

_____

_____

8. Why do you think Joshua tells the people what
   he does in 24:19-20 in response to 24:16-18?

_____

_____

_____

_____

_____

_____

Witnesses (24:22). It was necessary to have witnesses to attest any legal transaction, such as a
covenant or contract. The witnesses of this covenant were the people themselves and the stone
monument (24:22,26-27). The written record
was a kind of witness also. When Israel broke
the covenant later, the Lord was able to point to
the witnesses to prove the justice of His
punishment.

Buried (24:30,32,33). "Since it was a deep desire of
the ancients to be buried in their homeland,
these notices not only mark the conclusion of
the story and the close of an era but also
underscore the fact that Israel had indeed been
established in the promised homeland—the
Lord had kept His covenant."[2]

9. How would you describe the mood with which the book of Joshua ends in 24:25-33?

_____

_____

_____

_____

_____

_____

10. What do you think is the main message of chapter 24 . . .

for future generations of Israelites? _____

_____

_____

_____

_____

for us? _____

_____

_____

_____

_____

11. How is 24:1-33 relevant to you? What truth from it do you want to take to heart and apply?

_____

_____

_____

_____

_____

_____

Optional Application: a. Are you able to serve the Lord (24:19)? Do you choose to serve Him (24:14-15)? Pray about this, and come to a serious decision. How will your decision affect the way you lead your life from now on?

b. Memorize and reflect on 24:14-15.

12. What action can you take to put this truth into practice?

_____

_____

_____

_____

_____

_____

13. List any questions you have about chapter 24.

_____

_____

_____

_____

_____

For the group

Warm-up. Ask each person to name one thing God has done for him or her recently, one reason why he or she is thankful.

Read aloud. Have one person read the narrator's part (24:1,25-26,28-33), another be Joshua (24:2-15, 19-20,22a,23,27), and the rest read the people's parts (24:16-18,21,22b,24). Listen carefully to what you each say, and put yourselves into the scene. Let this meeting be a chance for each of you to renew your own commitments to the Lord.

Questions. Verse 19 is probably the toughest to grasp, so take some time to wrestle with questions 7 and 8. However, let your focus be on what the Lord has done for Israel and how Israel must respond, and then on what He has done for you and how you will respond. You might ask different people to explain in more detail what God did for Abraham, Jacob, and Israel under Moses, in case anyone is unfamiliar with those events.

Worship. Praise God for choosing and leading Abraham, for giving him sons, for liberating Israel from slavery in Egypt, for leading the people safely through the wilderness, for giving them victory after victory, and for giving them the land, the cities, the vineyards, and the groves. Praise Him for taking care of His people at every step. Worship Him as a holy and jealous God, and ask Him for the grace to abandon false gods and serve Him.

1. Woudstra, page 349.
2. *The NIV Study Bible*, page 324.

REVIEW

When you finish studying a book, it's a good idea to step back to look at it as a whole and see what you've learned. The best way to begin is to read the entire book quickly at one sitting. This will refresh your memory and draw your attention to themes that run through the chapters. Because Joshua is long, you might want to skim the land allotments.

1. What would you now say the book of Joshua is about? What does it contribute to the whole story of the Bible?

    _____

    _____

    _____

    _____

    _____

    _____

2. What does the book reveal about the following topics:

    God's nature _____

    _____

    _____

For Thought and Discussion: a. What are the general purposes of every Old Testament book (Romans 15:4, 1 Corinthians 10:11)?
b. How does Joshua fulfill those purposes?

God's priorities, values, aims, and methods _____

the covenant between God and Israel _____

Israel's inheritance _____

164

how Israel conquered the promised land _____

_____

_____

_____

_____

_____

_____

other themes _____

_____

_____

_____

_____

_____

_____

3. What truths did you learn from studying Joshua that are personally relevant to you?

_____

_____

_____

_____

_____

_____

_____

_____

_____

For Further Study:
Write a complete outline of the book of Joshua. Use any outlines you have already made, such as questions 5 and 6 of lesson one.

4. How have you changed (in attitudes and actions) as a result of your study of Joshua?

_____

_____

_____

_____

_____

_____

5. Look back through the study at questions in which you expressed a desire to make some application? Are you satisfied with your follow-through? In what areas would you like to continue to pursue growth, and how will you go about this?

_____

_____

_____

_____

_____

_____

_____

_____

6. Do any of the questions you listed at the ends of lessons one through fifteen remain unanswered? If so, copy them here, and plan ways to seek answers. Look for some of the resources named on pages 169-173, do some further Bible study on your own, or ask someone you trust.

_____

_____

_____

For the group

Reviewing a book can be vague and general because
people remember it only dimly or have difficulty
tying details together to see the big picture. Review
can also be a dull rehash of what people feel they
have already learned.

On the other hand, it can be an exciting
chance to see the story as God sees it, as a whole.
The keys to achieving this latter situation are the
attitudes of the leader and the group. The leader
needs to motivate the group to want to see the
God's-eye view. He or she needs to encourage
members who find it hard to connect ideas from
many chapters. He or she must also urge the group
to think deeply when quick answers seem to say
everything easily. At the same time, each group
member needs to discipline himself to think and
pray more deeply.

Warm-up. It might be motivating to ask, "What is
the most exciting thing you have learned about God
during the past four months from studying Joshua?"

Questions. Try to split your time evenly between
reviewing the content of the book (questions 1 and
2) and assessing how you have applied and want to
apply it (questions 3-5). Also, give everyone a chance
to ask about anything they still don't understand
(question 6). Encourage group members, rather
than the leader, to suggest or find answers so that
the group will grow less dependent on the leader.

When you review applications, try not to let
members compare their growth to each other's or to
focus on guilt and failure. If anyone feels he has
not obeyed God or grown much, you can discuss
whether that is true and how the person can
approach the situation from now on. Strive to
encourage one another.

Evaluation. You might set aside a whole meeting to evaluate your study of Joshua and plan where to go next. Here are some questions you might consider:

> How well did the study help you grasp the book of Joshua?
> What did you like best about your meetings?
> What did you like least? What would you change, and how?
> How well did you meet the goals you set at your first meeting?
> What did you learn about small group study?
> How could you practice together something you learned from your study?
> What are the members' current needs? What will you do next?

Worship. Praise God for revealing Himself to you through the book of Joshua. Thank Him for what He is doing in each of your lives. Ask Him to guide you as to where you should go from here.

STUDY AIDS

For further information on the material covered in this study, consider the following sources. Your local bookstore can order them if it does not carry them. Most seminary libraries and many university and public libraries will also carry them.

Commentaries on Joshua

Jensen, Irving L. *Joshua: Rest-Land Won* (Everyman's Bible Commentary, Moody Press, 1966).
> This is a brief but well-done exposition of Joshua. Jensen is excellent at overview and has some good ideas for application. Jensen is a thoroughly conservative evangelical.

Hamlin, E. John. *Joshua: Inheriting the Land* (International Theological Commentary, Eerdmans, 1983).
> This is a theological, rather than a critical, commentary. That is, instead of dealing with authorship, meanings of specific words, and so on, Hamlin focuses on the significance of the book for Israel and the modern Church. Hamlin has taught in Singapore and Thailand for most of his career, so he takes a Third World perspective that Western readers will find stimulating or frustrating or both, depending on their views. Also, Hamlin takes for granted the opinions of liberal-critical scholarship about authorship and date, so conservative readers may object to some of the conclusions he draws from those assumptions. Still, the work is a fine piece of scholarship and is worth reading with discernment.

Schaeffer, Francis A. *Joshua and the Flow of Biblical History* (InterVarsity, 1975).
> Schaeffer's main aim is to apply the lessons of Joshua to modern

life and worldview. Along the way, he brings the book alive by putting it into the context of the rest of Scripture and by fleshing out the scenes with cultural and geographical background. Like Jensen and Hamlin, this is not verse-by-verse commentary. Nevertheless, it is fun and inspiring reading, up to Schaeffer's standards.

Woudstra, Marten H. *The Book of Joshua* (New International Commentary on the Old Testament, Eerdmans, 1981).

This is probably the best verse-by-verse critical commentary around if you want a conservative evangelical approach. Woudstra has done a magnificent job dealing with liberal criticism while exegeting the text thoroughly. His work is quite readable for the layman and invaluable for the scholar.

Histories, Concordances, Dictionaries, and Handbooks

A *history* or *survey* traces Israel's history from beginning to end, so that you can see where each biblical event fits. *A Survey of Israel's History* by Leon Wood (Zondervan, 1970) is a good basic introduction for laymen from a conservative viewpoint. Not critical or heavily learned, but not simplistic. Many other good histories are available.

A *concordance* lists words of the Bible alphabetically along with each verse in which the word appears. It lets you do your own word studies. An *exhaustive* concordance lists every word used in a given translation, while an *abridged* or *complete* concordance omits either some words, some occurrences of the word, or both.

The two best exhaustive concordances are *Strong's Exhaustive Concordance* and *Young's Analytical Concordance to the Bible*. Both are available based on the King James Version of the Bible and the New American Standard Bible. *Strong's* has an index by which you can find out which Greek or Hebrew word is used in a given English verse. *Young's* breaks up each English word it translates. However, neither concordance requires knowledge of the original language.

Among other good, less expensive concordances, *Cruden's Complete Concordance* is keyed to the King James and Revised Versions, and *The NIV Complete Concordance* is keyed to the New International Version. These include all references to every word included, but they omit "minor" words. They also lack indexes to the original languages.

A *Bible dictionary* or *Bible encyclopedia* alphabetically lists articles about people, places, doctrines, important words, customs, and geography of the Bible.

The New Bible Dictionary, edited by J. D. Douglas, F. F. Bruce, J. I. Packer, N. Hillyer, D. Guthrie, A. R. Millard, and D. J. Wiseman (Tyndale, 1982) is more comprehensive than most dictionaries. Its 1300 pages include quantities of information along with excellent maps, charts, diagrams, and an index for cross-referencing.

Unger's Bible Dictionary by Merrill F. Unger (Moody, 1979) is equally good and is available in an inexpensive paperback edition.

The Zondervan Pictorial Encyclopedia edited by Merrill C. Tenney (Zondervan, 1975, 1976) is excellent and exhaustive, and is being revised and updated. However, its five 1000-page volumes are a financial investment, so all but very serious students may prefer to use it at a library.

Unlike a Bible dictionary in the above sense, *Vine's Expository Dictionary of New Testament Words* by W. E. Vine (various publishers) alphabetically lists major words used in the King James Version and defines each New Testament Greek word that KJV translates with that English word. *Vine's* lists verse references where that Greek word appears, so that you can do your own cross-references and word studies without knowing any Greek.

Vine's is a good basic book for beginners, but it is much less complete than other Greek helps for English speakers. More serious students might prefer *The New International Dictionary of New Testament Theology*, edited by Colin Brown (Zondervan) or *The Theological Dictionary of the New Testament* by Gerhard Kittel and Gerhard Friedrich, abridged in one volume by Geoffrey W. Bromiley (Eerdmans).

A **Bible atlas** can be a great aid to understanding what is going on in a book of the Bible and how geography affected events. Here are a few good choices:

The Macmillan Atlas by Yohanan Aharoni and Michael Avi-Yonah (Macmillan, 1968, 1977) contains 264 maps, 89 photos, and 12 graphics. The many maps of individual events portray battles, movements of people, and changing boundaries in detail.

The New Bible Atlas by J. J. Bimson and J. P. Kane (Tyndale, 1985) has 73 maps, 34 photos, and 34 graphics. Its evangelical perspective, concise and helpful text, and excellent research make it a very good choice, but its greatest strength is its outstanding graphics, such as cross-sections of the Dead Sea.

The Bible Mapbook by Simon Jenkins (Lion, 1984) is much shorter and less expensive than most other atlases, so it offers a good first taste of the usefulness of maps. It contains 91 simple maps, very little text, and 20 graphics. Some of the graphics are computer-generated and intriguing.

The Moody Atlas of Bible Lands by Barry J. Beitzel (Moody, 1984) is scholarly, very evangelical, and full of theological text, indexes, and references. This admirable reference work will be too deep and costly for some, but Beitzel shows vividly how God prepared the land of Israel perfectly for the acts of salvation He was going to accomplish in it.

A **handbook** of biblical customs can also be useful. Some good ones are *Today's Handbook of Bible Times and Customs* by William L. Coleman (Bethany, 1984) and the less detailed *Daily Life in Bible Times* (Nelson, 1982).

For Small Group Leaders

The Small Group Leader's Handbook by Steve Barker et al. (InterVarsity, 1982).
Written by an InterVarsity small group with college students primarily in mind. It includes information on group dynamics and how to lead in light of them, and many ideas for worship, building community, and outreach. It has a good chapter on doing inductive Bible study.

Getting Together: A Guide for Good Groups by Em Griffin (InterVarsity, 1982).
Applies to all kinds of groups, not just Bible studies. From his own experience, Griffin draws deep insights into why people join groups; how people relate to each other; and principles of leadership, decision-making, and discussions. It is fun to read, but its 229 pages will take more time than the above book.

You Can Start a Bible Study Group by Gladys Hunt (Harold Shaw, 1984).
Builds on Hunt's thirty years of experience leading groups. This book is wonderfully focused on God's enabling. It is both clear and applicable for Bible study groups of all kinds.

How to Build a Small Groups Ministry by Neal F. McBride (NavPress, 1994).
This hands-on workbook for pastors and lay leaders includes everything you need to know to develop a plan that fits your unique church. Through basic principles, case studies, and worksheets, McBride leads you through twelve logical steps for organizing and administering a small groups ministry.

How to Lead Small Groups by Neal F. McBride (NavPress, 1990).
Covers leadership skills for all kinds of small groups—Bible study, fellowship, task, and support groups. Filled with step-by-step guidance and practical exercises to help you grasp the critical aspects of small group leadership and dynamics.

DJ Plus, a special section in *Discipleship Journal* (NavPress, bimonthly).
Unique. Three pages of this feature are packed with practical ideas for small groups. Writers discuss what they are currently doing as small group members and leaders. To subscribe, write to Subscription Services, Post Office Box 54470, Boulder, Colorado 80323-4470.

Bible Study Methods

Braga, James. *How to Study the Bible* (Multnomah, 1982).
Clear chapters on a variety of approaches to Bible study: synthetic, geographical, cultural, historical, doctrinal, practical, and so on. Designed to help the ordinary person without seminary training to use these approaches.

Fee, Gordon, and Douglas Stuart. *How to Read the Bible For All Its Worth* (Zondervan, 1982).

After explaining in general what interpretation (exegesis) and application (hermneneutics) are, Fee and Stuart offer chapters on interpreting and applying the different kinds of writing in the Bible: Epistles, Gospels, Old Testament Law, Old Testament narrative, the Prophets, Psalms, Wisdom, and Revelation. Fee and Stuart also suggest good commentaries on each biblical book. They write as evangelical scholars who personally recognize Scripture as God's Word for their daily lives.

Jensen, Irving L. *Independent Bible Study* (Moody, 1963), and *Enjoy Your Bible* (Moody, 1962).

The former is a comprehensive introduction to the inductive Bible study method, especially the use of synthetic charts. The latter is a simpler introduction to the subject.

Wald, Oletta. *The Joy of Discovery in Bible Study* (Augsburg, 1975).

Wald focuses on issues such as how to observe all that is in a text, how to ask questions of a text, how to use grammar and passage structure to see the writer's point, and so on. Very helpful on these subjects.

YOU CAN LEAD DYNAMIC, LIFE-CHANGING SMALL-GROUP BIBLE STUDIES!

We hope you've enjoyed this NavPress study guide. Good materials are only part of what makes a successful and fulfilling small-group experience. That's why NavPress is pleased to announce PILGRIMAGE/NAVPRESS SMALL-GROUP TRAINING SEMINARS.

Whether you've led groups for years or are just starting out, PILGRIMAGE/NAVPRESS SMALL GROUP TRAINING will help you create and lead the kind of groups that foster life-changing spiritual growth.

In just 7 hours you'll learn:

> ▶ "Hands-on" small-group training techniques from the leading experts in North America

> ▶ The 7 essential skills every effective small-group leader needs

> ▶ How groups can specialize in worship, evangelism, discipleship, and emotional healing

> ▶ Plus, you'll receive group discounts on NavPress small-group resources, a comprehensive training manual, and two free study tools (*Learning to Love God* and *The Message: Psalms*)

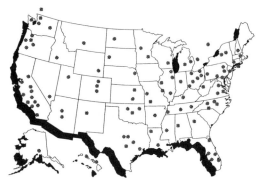

PILGRIMAGE/NAVPRESS SMALL-GROUP TRAINING SEMINARS are held at hundreds of locations all over North America. Call 1-800-GRPS-R-US for more information about seminars available in your area.

1-800-477-7787

PILGRIMAGE
NAVPRESS

Other titles in the
Lifechange series
you may be interested in: